CROSSING BORDERS

PARTNERS IN CRIME, THE SAN DIEGO CHAPTER OF SISTERS IN CRIME, PRESENTS

CROSSING BORDERS

EDITED BY
LISA BRACKMANN AND
MATT COYLE

Foreword by RACHEL HOWZELL HALL

Down & Out Books
3959 Van Dyke Road, Suite 265
Lutz, FL 33558
DownAndOutBooks.com

Cover design by Zach McCain

ISBN: 1-64396-079-2
ISBN-13: 978-1-64396-079-1

CONTENTS

FOREWORD

Rachel Howzell Hall

I'll never cheat.
I'll never become addicted.
I'll never kill another human being.

You've heard those words spoken.

You've witnessed those words become lies.

You've seen those lines crossed. In your own life. In a partner's life. A friend's. And that line-crosser, the one who swore to you *on their momma's grave* that they'd never do that thing? You've seen that person cross that line, step over that border, and disappear into a strange land. Sometimes, their return may be impossible. Sometimes, if they do make it back to you, back to that border, they're...*different* somehow. For good or not-so-good. Changed, though. Definitely.

Good stories start with characters crossing borders and finding themselves in worlds filled with hurt, harm, and danger. In *Crossing Borders*, the first anthology from Partners in Crime, the San Diego Chapter of Sisters in Crime, fifteen stories capture moments before, during and after characters cross borders and find themselves stumbling around strange lands that abound with saints, sinners, and monsters.

This short story collection explores all types of borders—

from crossing physical borders between states and countries, to crossing borders that separate life and death. Suspense, mystery, paranormal—this anthology crosses the genre border, too.

Be prepared to hold your breath, Dear Reader. And then? Make a run for the border.

See you there.

ONE FLU OVER THE CUCKOO'S NEST

Kathy Krevat

She was already dead.

To most, that fact wouldn't be remarkable. Angela Willis was an elderly-before-her-time woman in the advanced stages of lung cancer, activated by a secret smoking habit that even her deceased husband had never known about.

But I knew that her death had happened too early.

Because I was supposed to kill her.

My day began like any other. I traveled from hand to hand, blown through the air by a cough, then a sneeze, in a convoluted route of public buses, eighteen-wheeled behemoths, and inside a particularly fruitful family minivan with stickers on the back window, each with a child's name, the window just begging for an attack by a serial killer. It would have to settle for me. If I could feel pity, I'd have reserved some for the mother of the soon-to-be coughing, sneezing, and whining family.

Some would imagine that I was a simple virus, but they'd be dangerously wrong. I am the superhero of illness. A demigod of influenza. A first cousin to Death.

Not that he showed up at family reunions or anything.

Cincinnati had been suffocatingly hot, but spring had decided to stay in Winslow, Ohio past its checkout date. The people of the town seemed to be enjoying the weather. They certainly talked about it enough during my tour of the town's highlights—the 7-Eleven store and Target.

I jumped ship from my mom transport at the grocery store and used my extra sensory perception to find my next ride. Just kidding—I spotted the Udall Hospice Care Center employee badge clipped to the scrubs pocket on a customer behind me in the checkout line and waited on the keypad, a cesspool of bacteria and lesser viruses. Udall was my destination, and "Idalia Young," according to her badge, was going to get me there.

Idalia looked exactly like her name. Wide-eyed and fresh as a daisy. I lurked deep within the pad to avoid the elderly man she let in front of her with only one item.

"Good morning, Nancy," she said to the checkout lady in a perky tone that seemed to burst with the joy of living.

Even an ancient cynic like myself felt a stirring inside, like it might actually be a good day.

"Good morning, Idalia," the older woman replied. "Off to work?"

"Oh yes. Another day, another dollar." Idalia gave a little laugh.

The lack of originality was disappointing, but her enthusiasm was admirable.

Nancy didn't even bother looking in Idalia's brown bag from the deli to confirm its contents. "The usual?"

"Yep," Idalia said, as if that was just fine with her. "Same old, same old." She turned to punch in her telephone number on the keypad. Just as I was about to leap aboard my express shuttle, a stray sunbeam shone through the edge of the curtain shielding the customers, causing her brown hair to glow in a halo and lighting the gold flecks in her eyes.

I stopped still, entranced. What was wrong with me? I hadn't had feelings this strong since my massacre of 1918. I'd experienced what I believe humans feel on a roller coaster—the glee of my power had taken hold of me until absolute devastation had reigned. I'd kept myself in check, relatively, since then.

"Ham and cheese sandwich and large coffee." Nancy clicked away. "Four ninety-five."

Damn. I'd forgotten to jump. I scurried to the edge of the keypad, not wanting to miss my ride. I also didn't want to miss out on the experience of the delightful young lady.

"Here you go," Idalia said, handing over exact change instead of sliding her credit card.

It was like she knew what I was doing.

"Thanks so much," the clerk said. "You have a nice day at work, okay?"

"Hope so," Idalia said.

No! She moved past me, too far away to attempt anything drastic. I didn't understand the depths of my disappointment. What was wrong with me? I'd just have to wait for another potential lift.

"Don't forget your sandwich," Nancy said.

Idalia shook her head. "Silly me." She turned back and I lurched onto her sleeve as she grabbed the bag.

I held on tight and felt something entirely unfamiliar.

Happiness. Just being in the presence of such a cheerful, innocent person. The feeling was both foreign and recognizable. To a human, it would be the nostalgia of a long-lost memory, brought to life with a photograph.

I moved onto her arm, and the scent of her lemon and lavender soap filled my senses. Yes, I have senses. Not like humans, but I know lemon when I smell it.

Then I sensed something else. Alcohol residue. Idalia was fighting off a hangover.

And still so chipper. What an angel.

And then I went deeper. Was that an elevated level of leucocytes and nitrites? Ah, the beginnings of a bladder infection.

Alcohol plus a UTI? Maybe Idalia wasn't so innocent. Even better. Complex heroines are much more captivating.

Soon we were in an ancient Honda with a clattering catalytic converter—not quite a death rattle—and on our way. All too soon, she'd pulled into the parking lot behind the hospice, and it was time to do my job. From the outside, the center looked charming. A quaint, vaguely Victorian house, with rocking chairs on the wrap-around porch.

Before Idalia exited the car, she surprised me once again. She bowed her head, clasped her hands together and said, "God Almighty. I know in your infinite wisdom that your plans for my patients are just. Please help me to ease their pain and to make their journey toward you happy and joyful. Amen."

Someone like Idalia *would* be idealistic enough to believe in an omnipotent power. I couldn't help but believe that any god worth his salt would surely be busy curing Ebola (a rather nasty fellow) rather than deciding when a nobody in small town Ohio should die.

Idalia's phone dinged outside the Employee Only entrance and she pulled it out of her pocket. A text from Roger read, *Last night was awesome!*

Her heart started to race, and she smiled. Then she blew out a breath. "Play it cool," she whispered to herself, and I felt her heartbeat slow. Nice control. She typed out, *Had a great time!* along with a bunch of heart emojis. Her finger hovered over the phone and then she deleted all the hearts and the exclamation point before hitting Send. She turned off the sound and put it back in her pocket.

This girl knew how to play the game.

You wouldn't think I'd be a romantic but I am. A hopeless romantic. I've been known to hold off on my duty to see the outcome of an exchanged glance, a lingering touch, or a shuddering kiss.

I also love me some villains. Ooh, the chill of a jealous scowl, the attack of a vicious smile, or the calculation of a devious plan.

The endless ability of humans to cheat, steal, murder—to dehumanize—their fellow humans never ceases to fascinate me.

I'm also a bit of a birdwatcher.

The inside of the hospice looked just as charming as the outside, but the Fabreeze-esque attempts to mask the scent of approaching death had proved ineffectual. Fake flowers in plastic vases dotted the living room. The rose pattern on the sofa hid stains of patients' failing bladders and loosened bowels but could do nothing about the filth interred inside the cushions—never quite drying excrement that released its scent whenever an unsuspecting first-time guest made the unfortunate choice to sit down, never to make that mistake again.

Idalia stopped in the doorway of the employee lounge and greeted a tired woman who was clocking out with a cheerful, "Good morning!" She took her own timecard out of the slot.

The woman said, "Good night," with a smile, and left.

The lounge was a small room painted gray of all things, with a flickering fluorescent light, four chairs scavenged from the Salvation Army, and a plastic table typically used to sell counterfeit purses on street corners. A microwave sat on a tiny counter beside a deep utility sink, next to a small refrigerator.

A middle-aged man with "Harold" on his name tag gave Idalia a too loud, "Yo!" sounding like the *very* Jersey Shore part of New Jersey. He watched her bend over to put her lunch into the refrigerator, surreptitiously pulling at his crotch. A woman wearing a "Mabel" name tag came into the room and glared at him. He looked guilty enough for me to realize they had a relationship, if not a marriage, between them.

Mabel tried and failed to quell her expression of resentment of Idalia, most likely due to the girl's youth and what Mabel assumed was a glowing future that didn't involve bedpans. "Quick turnaround for you." She may have been trying to be friendly, but it came out sarcastically, as if she couldn't help herself. "Didn't you just work until midnight?"

"I don't mind," Idalia said.

Mabel left without a word. Idalia washed her hands at the sink and put on her latex gloves. She smiled at the woman at the "Nurse Station" and paged through standing folders marked with employee names. Inside was her list of patients, with Angela Willis at the bottom.

My assignment.

I knew I had to fulfill my duty, but I already felt a loss from having to move on from Idalia. She walked down to the end of the hall, right into Angela's room.

Wait! So soon?

"Good morning," Idalia said in a sing-song voice until she got a good look at her patient.

Angela was already dead. How was this possible? She was supposed to die of *me*.

Idalia recognized the obvious right away, slapping the emergency button as she cried, "Oh no!" Her heart began pounding.

Mabel came running from the next room, as fast as her large size could bring her.

If I hadn't been so astonished myself—after all, Angela was *my* assignment—I might have paid more attention to their reactions. My plan had been to travel down one of Angela's many tubes, leak into her blood stream, and whirl to her lungs where my presence would be revealed. The lungs would ineffectively fight back, the resulting inflammation stopping the work of her bronchi. The coup de grâce would be a massive fluid buildup that would make breathing impossible. Death would have been mercifully swift at that point.

Instead, she was already gone. This hadn't occurred to me

in decades.

The inexplicable mystery intrigued me. I certainly could have taken the credit and moved on. But it had been so long since my boredom had been so effectively dislodged that I couldn't help myself.

I ran along the bed rail and jumped to Angela's hand. I scanned her as best I could, given that none of her functions were functioning, and sensed that something was off. I centered my chakras and used my psychic abilities to—I'm kidding. I've been in so many human bodies that I can tell a lot about a person by taking a dip into their skin and bloodstream. I could even translate the chemical building blocks of emotions.

That's me. A viral tricorder.

Poor Angela's bloodstream had already turned into a swampy mess of coagulation, with an overload of toxins from chemotherapy and, most interesting, an obvious overdose of insulin.

This woman had been killed. Was it gross negligence or deliberate?

If I could figure out who had administered the insulin, I could solve my little mystery and be on my way.

I followed the drip line to the IV clamp and tried to figure out who was the last to touch it. Unfortunately, the residue of too many hands clung to it, evidence that this place was a petri dish of reused gloves and other unfollowed health precautions.

From that viewpoint I took stock of the room. Fresh flowers stood on a short counter against the wall, with a standard notecard, saying, "Get Well Soon, Your loving son, John," perched on a plastic stand. A teddy bear sat beside it, all but announcing "Nanny Cam" to the world.

Whoa. The camera was turned toward the side of the room, where it could record only the wall.

I was already thinking that the most obvious suspects were employees of the hospice, but this solidified it. I tried to cast aside the unlikely idea that Idalia was capable of murder, but in the interests of being thorough, I grabbed onto her skin for a short scan. Nothing but dismay and a strong desire to pee.

I moved to Mabel.

Whew. Mabel needed a shower. She oozed regret and anger, and perhaps guilt. Emotion isn't an exact science.

"I'll let Wally know." Mabel tried to infuse sadness into her voice, but only sounded worried. "She'll want to notify the judge."

Judge?

I rode along as Mabel detoured to the employee lounge where Harold still sat, even though he had punched in, eating a tuna fish sandwich from the kitchen.

"She's dead," Mabel said accusingly.

"Who?"

"Angela Willis!"

"Already?" He jumped up, alarmed.

"Yes!"

"Did you—?"

"Sh!" She stuck her head out the door to make sure no one could hear.

My eyebrows rose, metaphorically at least. How intriguing.

"It wasn't me," she said.

"It wasn't *me*," he said.

"Goddammit," she said. "You go tell him right now it was you."

His face actually turned white. "But what if—?" Who was he so afraid of?

"What if—nuthin!'" She grabbed his arm and shoved him out the door. "I'll tell Wally you're sick and going home."

"I don't have any sick time," he protested.

"You tell him you done it and get the money and you won't need no sick time."

Much as my heart broke over the poor grammar from these pitiful examples of English language users, I listened with rapt attention.

Who was "he?" And what money was she talking about?

Before I could leap onto Harold, he was out the door. I'm embarrassed to admit that I even tried to jump and missed completely, landing in an undignified face plant on the scarred plastic chair.

I scrabbled back onto Mabel whose scent had become even more unpleasant with the addition of fear.

She hustled down the hallway, through the utilitarian kitchen, which was humid with the result of boiling potatoes and onions, and knocked on the door of what had once been a storage room. Cigarette smoke leaked from around the door, in spite of the "Udall Hospice Care Center is a Smoke-Free Environment" signs.

A rail-thin, sixty-something woman opened the door, waving her hand around at the smoke. This must be Wally.

"Angela Willis has passed," Mabel told her. "I thought you'd want to tell her family."

Wally's eyes widened. "Shit."

Mabel became defensive. "Well, she's been close to the end for *ages*," she said. "They can't be surprised."

Wally tugged at the bottom of her jacket, a vintage Dior that probably fit the era of most of her patients. "I'll take care of the notification." She slammed the door.

Mabel leaned a hand on the wall, taking a deep breath, and I ran down her arm, crawled down the doorjamb and entered the tiny office.

Wally slid into her desk chair and pulled a cell phone out of her purse. Since an iPhone with a neon pink cover sat prominently on her desk, I suspected that the one in her hand was a burner phone. I moved as fast as I could along the wall and hopped onto her desk.

She dialed a number by heart and waited for someone to answer.

I scooted up her arm to her earlobe.

Someone answered the phone but didn't say anything.

"It's done," she said, and hung up.

Ooh. I was riveted.

Then she picked up the pink cell, garishly decorated with crystals, what people call "bling" these days, and dialed a number listed under the name, "Wence at morgue." How odd.

"This is Wence," he answered.

I giggled inside.

"Patient number 476," Wally said. "Protocol 1."

"Will do," he said, a little too cheerfully for someone who had just been told that someone had died.

Wally hung up, swiped through the contacts to "Asshole," and hit the phone icon to dial.

"Asshole" answered with an impatient, "Yes."

"Mr. Summersby?" she said. "I wanted to let you know the unfortunate news that Angela Willis passed away early this morning. Would you like to handle the notification of her son or would you like me to do it?"

There was silence on the other end, as if he were evaluating a variety of scenarios.

After a moment, she asked, "Mr. Summersby?"

"You may call," he said, and hung up. None of society's niceties for either one of these two.

Wally let out a breath that was more relief than annoyance, pulled a file folder from a desk drawer and opened it. Then she used the office phone to dial the number beside "Next of kin."

John D. Willis, JD. The loving son. This must be the judge that Mabel mentioned.

"Ms. Wally Long for Judge Willis," she told the woman who answered. She waited for a moment. "Mr. Willis, I'm afraid I have some bad news."

The judge accepted the news stoically. "Thank you for letting me know."

I suddenly wished I could travel through the phone, like a cyber virus, to see what he did next.

But then Wally picked up a lethal looking letter opener,

stood up, and locked her door. I was right where I needed to be.

She opened her file cabinet, stood on her tiptoes and pulled the file folders toward the front. Then she jimmied open a barely perceptible trap door at the back with the letter opener, pulling out what looked like an old-fashioned accounting ledger.

She stuck it in her oversized burgundy bag and rushed out the back door of the hospice. I had a birds-eye view on her shoulder as she got into her ancient Kia. Her smoking-induced asthmatic breathing became little moaning heaves as she threw the car into reverse and turned the wheel. She zoomed out of the employee parking lot. "Too soon, too soon, too soon," she muttered over and over in a curious mixture of prayer and hopeless certainty that all was lost.

She forced a merge onto the two-lane road that backed up to the hospice center, and I watched with rapt attention as she darted into the other lane and wrenched the car back, narrowly avoiding an oncoming car that wasn't backing down. She drove like a NASCAR driver without any of the finesse.

Within minutes, she'd driven into a parking garage, all the way to the bottom floor. She grabbed her bag and got out, brushing by a shiny black SUV and almost dislodging me. I landed in an even more unpleasant position on her knee, gainfully clinging to her support hose. She yanked on her skirt and it covered me so I couldn't see anything but the ground.

Wally walked into the bowels of a dim stairwell that reeked of urine.

Then she gave a short cry and fell to the ground, and I heard someone running away. It took me ages to slide out between her limp skin and the damp cement. Her attacker was long gone, and he'd taken her bag. What was in it?

Wally moaned and a few minutes later, a middle-aged woman looked over the railing and gasped. Within minutes of calling 911, an ambulance appeared. I hitched a ride to the hospital.

***

After a whirlwind of activity in the ER, Wally was settled in a curtained cubicle, asleep. Mabel sat in the plastic chair beside her, seeming not quite sure why she was there.

A detective walked into the room, took one look at the unconscious Wally, and zeroed in on Mabel. He was in his fifties and had a lot of muscle under a small beer belly, like the flab was simply camouflage.

He introduced himself to Mabel—Detective Duke Bailey—and asked her the usual questions: name, relationship to the patient, what she knew about the assault.

"It doesn't make any sense," Mabel said. "She's a manager at a hospice center. She takes care of people." Sweat formed on her upper lip.

The detective's eyes glanced at the sweat. His expression didn't change but I could tell his interest in Mabel skyrocketed. "Anyone have a grudge against her?"

Mabel answered with a too emphatic, "No," and then added weakly, "Not that I know of."

"Really?" He sounded mildly skeptical. "She's never had an employee who didn't like her for no good reason other than she's the boss?"

"No." Her eyes slid away.

He waited.

She didn't rise to the bait.

Detective Bailey gave a heavy sigh, trying The Disappointment Approach. "We have to get in front of this, before someone else is hurt. Or killed. And I think you can help."

"I don't know anything," she said.

He narrowed his eyes. "Here's what's gonna happen. I'm going to interview every single employee Ms. Wally has or had in the last, say, five years. And if any of them tell me that you knew of someone who had a problem with her, then I'm going to bring you to the station and charge you with obstruction of justice. Do you know what that is?"

Ooh. Bad Cop. I hopped onto the sleeve of his sports coat and headed up to his face, wanting to see what he saw.

She met his eyes, and even the detective could smell her perspiration from across the room. "Maybe Malcolm Salem?"

The detective wrote the name in his notebook. "What's his beef?"

She seemed almost grateful to give him somewhere to go with his inquiries. "Wally fired him a month ago. They had a big blowout in front of some of the staff."

"Who?"

"Louise Cardinal, the night nurse," she said. "And Idalia Young."

I felt a quiver at her name.

"Anyone else?" he asked.

"Not that I can think of," she said. "I'm just in shock about this and not thinking clearly."

He raised his eyebrows, which were impressively bushy, but let her get away with the evasion.

"Is it okay if I go?" she asked. "I should probably see if they need me at Udall."

"Yes," he said. "Do not discuss this with any of the other employees."

Did he really think anyone follows an order like that?

Which of these humans should I follow? As much as I'd love to see Idalia again, the best source of information was the detective.

After Mabel scurried off, Detective Duke took one look at Wally as if disgusted that she was unconscious and not helping his investigation. He stepped into the hall and placed a call on his cell. "Hey. Anything going on today? This attack can't be random."

"Nothing juicy," the man on the other end said. "Just an old lady with cancer."

Hmm. Was that *my* old lady with cancer?

"Okay." He seemed about to hang up.

No! How could I get him to ask about Angela? I moved to his neck and dove into a hair follicle, forcing it to rise. Its neighbors joined in like a bunch of lemmings. Then a visible chill ran down the detective's neck.

"Wait," he said. "Tell me about that old lady."

"She was a patient at the Udall Hospice Center, so nothing suspicious. Wence is taking the body straight to the crematorium. Not sure what the rush is," he said.

I furiously went to work again, causing another chill. "You call off that cremation," Duke said. "I got a feeling about this. I want a full autopsy."

The next day, I was reunited with Idalia. I'd had a lot of boring time to daydream about her, while Detective Duke interviewed a slew of suspects. Poor Malcolm got the worst treatment but had a rock-solid alibi of being on security cameras at a bordello, to say it politely.

The detective had visited Judge John Willis, but while the not-so-grief-stricken son noted that he had many enemies, he couldn't imagine how hurrying his mother's impending death along a few days faster helped anyone. I'd shuffled through a few papers on the judge's desk and found nothing of interest, except an apparent tobacco chewing habit. Disgusting.

The preliminary autopsy report noted the elevated levels of insulin, and the detective returned to Udall, wanting to know who had administered it. He'd viewed the nanny cam video and saw that two days before Angela died, Idalia had been cleaning and had replaced the bear in a different spot, facing the wall.

"Ms. Young," my buddy Duke said. "Are you familiar with nanny cams?"

They met in the employee break room. It took me forever to reach her hand, across a sea of mottled plastic. She was perfectly calm, her heartbeat and nervous system not reacting at all to his questions. Definitely innocent. On the other hand, Harold couldn't help but listen at the door, his heart pounding out of his chest and his body odor pooling along the floor and creeping in like a fetid fog. I couldn't trigger the detective's "intuition" without pointing to Idalia.

"Of course," she said. "But I've never seen one in person."

He held up the smiling bear in question. "Not even this one?"

She put her finger to her chin. The artificiality of it gave me pause and I could almost see the detective's detecting antenna rise. "That does look familiar."

She answered the rest of his questions calmly. No, she didn't know Ms. Willis's son was a judge. No, she had no idea why someone would want to hurt her. No, she would never do such a thing herself. Me, the ultimate lie detector test, detected nothing to indicate she was lying. Whew!

I phased out, enjoying her innocence and her peculiar scent of lemon and lavender, today mixed in with antibiotics to combat the infection. Then I sensed something deep underneath her surface calm. I dipped in and in a manner of speaking lifted my finger to the wind of her deepest emotions.

Anger. Burning hot, raging anger.

Interesting.

The detective finished, warning Idalia not to leave town, like a sheriff from an old movie. As soon as she got outside the hospice, she whipped her phone out of her pocket and I saw what she was upset about. Roger had stopped answering her texts. He hadn't responded to a whole page of them.

She got in her car, hit the phone icon, and hit redial. The "Roger Office" phone number had a twenty-two beside it. She'd called him at work twenty-two times? A woman answered with a long name of the law firm.

Law firm?

Then the nice lady told my poor Idalia that Roger no longer

worked at the company.

What trickery was this?

Idalia, ever polite, thanked the woman and hung up. Then she pounded the steering wheel with the heel of her hands over and over. Finally, breathless, she stopped. She shook out her hands and started the car.

She drove calmly toward Cincinnati, pulling off the highway when office buildings started popping up. She parked outside a four-story building and waited. Her eyes stayed on the front door.

A young man came out of the building and she gasped. This must be Roger. He was not at all what I expected, certainly not the insanely handsome suitor this gorgeous creature deserved. He was slight of frame and stature, bespectacled, with short brown hair trimmed meticulously above his tiny ears.

She was after Roger in a flash, catching him in the parking lot before he reached his car.

"Why haven't you returned my calls?" Idalia demanded, her normally delightful tones now an objectionable screech.

Roger put up his hands as if avoiding a slap. "I told you we have to lay low." He looked around wildly. "We can't be seen together, especially here."

She moved in close, pointing her finger close to his face. "You're dumping me? After what you made me do?"

What? I had to admit that she looked positively murderous.

Roger's eyes widened.

"Don't even think about getting rid of me." Her voice had dropped an octave.

"You got plenty of money to do it." His voice shook.

Such an amateur.

"I did it because I loved you," she said. "You slept with me. You used me!"

"I didn't." He stuttered. Clearly, he did and regretted only that she was confronting him.

My soul, such as it is, filled with abject disappointment.

My darling was clearly the murderer of Angela Willis, even it if was at the behest of her lover. Whatever was I to do?

Idalia stalked back to her car. Her pulse went back to normal. I dove deep and could find no hint of remorse or guilt.

My crush was a stone-cold killer.

It took me several days to clean up the mess. Detective Duke had a sudden sneezing fit, drawing his attention to a news article highlighting a lawsuit being brought by Roger's law firm. He checked his files and made the connection that Roger was Idalia's boyfriend.

The detective brought Roger in for questioning and he folded like a cheap suit, implicating Idalia and his law partner, who wanted to ensure that this particular lawsuit would be heard by a more sympathetic judge. Not fully trusting Roger's efforts, the partner had also hired Mabel, Harold, and Wally to do the same thing. He had been right not to trust Roger—Idalia had jumped the gun and killed Angela a few days too early. By the time they filed the lawsuit, Judge Willis was back at work.

When Idalia heard that Roger had been arrested, she emptied her bank account and hopped a bus to Los Angeles, eluding her own arrest.

Unfortunately for her, I'm not known for my forgiveness and came along for the ride.

Soon enough, I'd exact my own form of justice.

A KILLING IN BOGOTÁ 1995

Carl Vonderau

Chepe Ramirez couldn't remember when he had started fearing traffic jams. A year had passed since Pablo Escobar fell and only one thing had changed: the killers had stopped using bombs and gone back to guns and knives. He'd just exited the Autopista del Norte and the cars in front of him had congealed into a honking mass around the roundabout. He looked down at his hands. They clenched the steering wheel of his Oltcit.

He listened for the whine of a motorbike lifting above the traffic noise. The hawkers selling oranges and packs of Marlboros would see it knife through the spaces between cars. They'd scurry for cover, crossing themselves as the passenger behind the driver raised his Tech-9. Chepe wondered if he'd hear the pop and crackle of the machine gun.

He sucked in a long breath through his nose. The jitter in his hand was spreading to his arm and he was sweating. Paranoia had kicked in like a bout of malarial fever. He told himself that every faceless prosecutor caught this sickness eventually. The more successful they were, the more they twitched and shuddered. And the best ones? Their caskets were usually closed.

Chepe pushed the button for the Oltcit's cassette player. Gloria Estefan's deep voice filled the car. The Cuban dance rhythms always settled his arms and hands. He told himself that he'd be home in an hour. Home to Maria.

In front, a vendor flipped and re-spooled a Chinese-made Yo-Yo. On his left, another sold Mont Blanc knockoffs. Inside the little booth on the traffic island, a policeman filled out paperwork. A block away, a traffic cop in an orange vest limply waved his arms at the unmoving block of vehicles. Chepe slowly unclamped his hands from the steering wheel.

A street boy raised a sponge to his windows. "No," Ramirez shouted and waved his finger. But the *gamín* only stared ahead at the large wiper in the center of the Oltcit's windshield. Why not? Chepe decided. The traffic horns had melded into a single enraged bellow. No one would move anytime soon.

He shifted and the transmission ground into Park. As usual, the engine spluttered but tonight it stayed alive. He shook his head at yet another Colombian irony. He was prosecuting a *capo* worth billions of pesos and couldn't afford a new car.

It was late afternoon, his favorite time of day. Above Bogotá, the trees on the eastern cordillera glowed in dark, calming shades of green. Monserrate Church, shining white on the peak, hadn't changed since he was a child. Only Bogotá, the city below, had transmuted.

He thought of the interview that morning. A one-way mirror had hidden Chepe's face, and he'd used his codename. Still, he'd had the feeling the *capo* recognized his voice through the electronic distortion. It was the way the man smiled. As if he knew that Chepe was the faceless prosecutor behind the glass.

The *gamín* had clambered onto the hood to reach the middle of the windshield. Soot covered his face. His jacket—maybe it used to be plaid—was caked with mud from the sewers where he must have slept to keep warm. His brown pants were shot full of holes. Only the boy's red woven bag had somehow remained unsoiled.

Another irony, Chepe thought. Maria wept every month at their failure to conceive, while a few kilometers away, families abandoned their children. Maybe this *gamín* could work on one of the *capo's* buildings. Was that so bad? Escobar had helped the poor much more than any government. Chepe's long sigh hissed through the horns and shouts of the vendors. He thought of what Maria had said to him the night before. "Your idealism is as broken down as your car."

The boy jumped from the hood and scurried to the other side of the Oltcit. The windows he'd cleaned were dirtier than the ones he'd missed. His body looked like that of a nine- or ten-year-old, but his dark face bore the expression of someone years older.

He ran to Chepe's side of the car. His blackened cheeks cracked into a jumble of dimples, his teeth gleaming white by comparison. Who could resist a face like that? Chepe reached into his suit pocket for his wallet and withdrew five hundred pesos. It was too much, but he didn't care. He rolled down the window just as the *gamín* stuck his hand into his red sack. The boy pulled out a nine-millimeter pistol.

Chepe stared first at the handgun in the little hand, then at the twitching face. The boy pushed his pistol hand through the opening between the glass and the roof. He aimed the barrel at Chepe Ramirez's head.

"*Tranquilo,*" Chepe said.

The boy's hand shook.

Chepe slowly proffered his wallet toward the open window. He heard Gloria's voice. She'd moved on to a ballad about love.

The boy's mouth trembled as if he were fighting off tears.

Chepe smiled, his eyes soft.

A hole opened in Chepe Ramirez's temple.

***

The traffic cop in the glowing orange vest spotted the Oltcit stopped in traffic. An urchin had pulled open the car door and was scrambling around inside. Another damn *gamín* thief, he thought. What had happened to the driver?

The policeman in the Plaza Metropolitana guard house spotted the traffic cop in the orange vest running from his post. He saw the *gamín* scampering toward the Uniroyal station on Carrera 15. Men stood outside their cars and pointed at the motionless Oltcit. The policeman stepped out of his guard house and jogged toward the traffic cop and the *gamín*. What had this street kid stolen?

The policeman and the traffic cop converged on the boy in front of the office building next to the Uniroyal station. The guard from the building crept up from behind. An iron sewer grate stood open.

The policeman slid his pistol out of the holster and aimed. But he couldn't bring himself to shoot a child. Not for another petty theft. The last he saw of the boy was his red sack disappearing into the hole to the sewer.

By the time the three men looked into the opening, the urchin had disappeared. They glanced at one another and each shook his head. No one was paid enough to climb into the muck below. Not to chase a *gamín*.

"He shot the driver in the Oltcit," the traffic cop said.

"You should have killed the little shit," the building guard said.

On the other side of the roundabout, the people at the American-style roast beef shop gazed at the crowd and ate their sandwiches. A server stepped out to the sidewalk to stare. She still had on her black apron with the picture of the bull wearing a napkin.

Only one man knew which car to look at. His reflective sunglasses never wavered from the blue Oltcit just below the billboard of the Marlboro cowboy. As he stared at it, his thin, crevassed cheeks worked on the tough roast beef of the sandwich, gold front teeth glinting with each bite. He noted that no one pushed inside the car to help the victim. That meant the driver was dead. He swiveled his sunglasses to the policeman, then the traffic cop, and the security guard. They were trudging empty-handed from the sewer.

The man threw the sandwich onto the sidewalk and trudged away from the roundabout. He pulled out a pack of Marlboros from his leather jacket and lit one. After a block, he climbed into the passenger seat of a black Ford Bronco. He checked the time through the glass-covered hole in the top of his pocket watch. Taking out a cellular phone, he dialed a number to pass on the good news.

It was the policeman's job to examine the body lying on the seat. A bright red stream of blood oozed from the front of the man's head. The policeman studied his grey wool suit for signs of breathing. None. He retreated to the pavement and sat down. The street boy's wiper and bottle for cleaning the windshield lay beside the car. He'd dropped them so he could aim the pistol. "A child did this," he said. "A child."

"*Gamín hijo de puta*," the building guard said.

The traffic cop threw his orange vest onto the torn-up asphalt. "I hate this job."

A few blocks away, beside the old canvas tents selling baskets and flowers, the black Ford Bronco stopped by the curb and the thin man in the brown leather jacket jumped down. He levered the grate out of the cement sewer foundation. The boy with the red sack crawled out.

"*Vamos,*" the man said.

The boy trudged slowly toward the jeep.

After twenty meters, the man in the leather jacket turned and surveyed the vendors on the street. No one stood near them. "Do you have the gun?"

The boy nodded.

"A head shot?"

The boy's face bunched, new cracks splitting open in the dirt around his mouth. He squinted at the man in the leather jacket.

"Only girls and children cry," the man said. His eyes were hidden behind the silver ovals of his sunglasses.

The black Bronco turned back and edged through the stacks of cars onto the Autopista del Norte. In the back seat, the shooter, Antonio, was shaking. He pressed his mouth shut to stop his teeth from chattering. He held the pistol inside the red bag, feeling the warmth slowly dissipate from the barrel.

After a few blocks, Antonio pulled a fruit juice bottle and a white plastic bag from his sack. He poured Boxer glue into the sack and covered his face with the bag up to his cropped hair. The plastic contracted. He removed his head, exhaled, and stuck his face back inside.

The driver watched him through the rearview mirror. He nodded at the thin man in the leather jacket beside him in the front seat. The thin man took off his sunglasses and turned. He stared at Antonio through the space between the cargo seats. "You did very well."

Antonio lowered his head back into the bag.

"You don't need that now," the thin man in the leather jacket said. "We have plans for you."

Antonio lifted his face from the bag. White tears streaked his soot-blackened cheeks. "What plans?"

"You'll see," the thin man, Gustavo, said. His smile was full of gold.

* * *

Antonio smelled the wood and leather of Gustavo's cologne. It was so different from the sweet perfume his mother used to put on. The Bronco turned east on Jimenez and stopped beside the lines of stalls. Gustavo jumped to the sidewalk and motioned Antonio to follow.

Gustavo headed down Jimenez. Antonio walked two meters behind. He took in Gustavo's fancy jacket, the movie-star shoes with white webbing on the toes. The late afternoon sun was sinking, and Gustavo had left his sunglasses in the Bronco. He looked straight ahead as if nothing on that street could frighten him.

They passed through the jumble of buses on Carrera 10 and stopped beside a traffic cop blowing his whistle. Gustavo cut over to Calle 12 and the tin-roofed stalls of clothes. Gustavo stopped beside the best stall. Its bright lights showcased the merchandise even before it was dark.

"*A la órden,*" the vendor said.

Gustavo grabbed a pair of new Levi jeans and gazed back at Antonio. "Do you like white or blue?"

Antonio stayed back from the table. That way the vendor wouldn't think he was there to steal.

But he was with Gustavo. Antonio took a step closer. "Blue," he said.

The vendor looked him up and down and his eyes didn't slit up. Not a single threat. The vendor picked out a smaller pair of pants. He and Gustavo chose a long-sleeved rugby shirt and a gray canvas jacket. Antonio wondered what Gustavo wanted in return for these clothes. It was best not to ask. Not now.

Gustavo gave the vendor some pesos. The vendor nodded and put the clothes in the plastic sack. Gustavo turned and whistled as he walked, swinging the sack at his side. Antonio followed a safe few meters behind. Gustavo walked to the other side of Calle 12 and past more wooden booths selling clothes. He stopped under a dirty plastic awning. Hundreds of tennis shoes lined the red metal table and wooden shelves.

"Nike?" the vendor asked.

Antonio nodded and edged to the side of the booth. He slipped off his own shoes. They were held together with wire. He tried on five pairs until Gustavo found some high-tops that fit just right. The shoes snuggled Antonio's feet and made him feel warm. No one would catch him now.

"*A la órden.*" The vendor looked at Antonio when he said it.

They walked back to Jimenez Street, its packs of busses farting black gusts of diesel. Gustavo led him past long lines of people waiting to go home. People who slept in houses with beds and who covered themselves with blankets instead of newspapers.

They reached the black Bronco. The street was now lit up for the night, but the driver still waited. Gustavo pulled his watch from his pocket as gently and carefully as a king's jewel. Instead of getting in the SUV, they wriggled through the crowd between the stores and the stalls.

He walked so close. Antonio could have touched the plastic bag, then the fine leather of Gustavo's brown jacket. Tonight the street sounded happy—the radios blasting *cumbias* and the vendors shouting hoarsely. The traffic cops grinned at girls and blew their whistles.

Gustavo stopped beside a stall with a canvas tarp for a roof. The owner was reading a book under a bare lightbulb. "What is *Macroeconomía?*" Antonio asked.

"You can read," Gustavo said. "That's good."

Antonio stared at the plastic-wrapped magazines hanging from a clothesline around the yellow walls—row after row of every kind of breast and buttock lit up by a green cord of lights.

"We have men, too," the man with the book said.

Gustavo's eyes widened. "Do you think we're *maricones?*" His voice was as quiet as a knife.

"No, no, of course not," the vendor said. "I didn't mean to

suggest..." His gaze fell back to his book. He swallowed.

Gustavo stared at the man's bowed head. The traffic horns and shouts of other vendors rose around them. He turned. Antonio read his eyes. *Never let anyone even* hint *you're like that.*

Antonio leaned against the chipped wooden counter beside Gustavo and took in the girl on each cover. He'd never looked at so many wide butts and big *tetas.* Gustavo pointed to a magazine with a blonde *gringa.* The owner looked up from his book. Gustavo gave him some money and slipped the magazine into the plastic bag with the clothes.

This was all for him. Antonio was sure of it. It was his payment for shooting the man in the ugly car.

Farther down Avenida Caracas, a boy Antonio knew limped like a shadow between the belching cars and buses. He thrust out a plastic cup.

"Not everyone gets an opportunity," Gustavo said.

They passed a woman grilling sausages on a spittle. Antonio sucked in a deep breath. Gustavo turned into one of the little restaurants. Antonio stopped. The owners would never let him inside. Gustavo would be embarrassed.

"You're with me," Gustavo said and motioned him to follow.

He led Antonio past the display case, sugar bread piled up inside its glass sides. They strode across the orange-tiled floor to a table in the back near the kitchen. Orange shelves full of beer and soft drinks and *aguardiente* stood beside them.

"Sit," Gustavo said.

Antonio glanced at the broad-faced woman in the white apron. She was big-hipped like his mother, but without the smile. She stared at his grimy jacket and tattered pants. Her eyes seemed to latch onto his pure white high-tops with new laces. The woman didn't tell him not to sit. He dropped into the chair across and drew in the smell of cooking meat.

"*Dos tintos,*" Gustavo said to her.

The girl in the back put down her broom and fixed a scarf. Her black hair was long and thick and overflowed the red fabric. She disappeared behind the counter. Pots and pans banged and chimed.

Antonio smiled. A beautiful girl was making him coffee.

Beside him, Gustavo sniffed as if even this café were not good enough. He wore a shirt without a single stain. The bright pink and white stripes seemed to beam out the scents of his leather jacket and cologne.

The coffee came in little white porcelain cups with three sugars. While they stirred, Gustavo yelled, "*Arroz con pollo.*"

"*Sí, señor,*" the wide-hipped woman in the white apron said.

Expensive rice and chicken. Antonio watched the woman bustle back behind the counter. Gustavo's face looked as if he expected no less. Gustavo, who had never hit him. Not even once. Not like his mother's new man.

"Did you find anything in the car?" Gustavo asked.

Antonio shook his head.

"No papers or envelopes? Nothing in the back seat?"

He seemed disappointed. Now he was going to start yelling. Those clean fingers would curl into a fist.

Gustavo reached across the table and patted him on the shoulder. "Don't worry." He stirred another sugar into the *tinto* and sipped. His eyes rose from the cup to fix on him. An adult's question lurked behind that stare. Antonio looked away.

"Did your father leave your mother?" Gustavo asked.

Antonio said nothing.

"He couldn't find work?"

Antonio shrugged his shoulders.

"He was on *bazuco,* wasn't he?"

How did Gustavo know? Did he also know where his father was now, lying all day on a black plastic garbage bag in Cartucho?

"That's what your friends will do soon. When they have more money, they'll buy *bazuco.*"

"Boxer is cheaper."

Gustavo shook his head. "It will rot your brain. Five years, maximum."

Antonio snickered. In five years, he'd be dead.

"So your mother got a new man."

Gustavo was blaming his mother. But she had tried to protect him. She would never be the bad one. "We needed money," Antonio said.

"And the new man beat you and forced you onto the street. Didn't he?"

Antonio stared into the dark coffee. It shined on the top. Beside him, Gustavo's metal spoon scraped against his cup. Antonio didn't like how much Gustavo knew about his mother. His feet shifted in the new Nike high-tops. He could run out the door. In ten minutes, he'd be back laughing with Little Tucho and Ratón. They'd share their Boxer.

"I'm going to the country tomorrow," Gustavo said. "Have you ever been outside of Bogotá?"

"Soacha," Antonio said.

Gustavo laughed. "That's not the country. You drive past the Falls of Tequendama and down the mountains. One more hour and the land totally changes. You see trees everywhere and the air smells clean. Wild orchids grow beside streams. The water is clear. I'll take you there one day. You can see a little bit of what Colombia used to look like."

The gold inside Gustavo's mouth was covered up, but his eyes shone.

"Someday you and I will buy *fincas* there," Gustavo said. "Your house will be next to mine."

Antonio drew in the woody leather smell of Gustavo's cologne. He squeezed the porcelain handle of the coffee cup. He imagined birds singing in tree branches full of green leaves. Water lapping in front of him. His mother splashing in his very own swimming pool. *Antonio, come in the water.*

He reached into his sack. He felt the gun, then the wallet.

He put the wallet on the table.

Gustavo opened it. "Chepe Ramirez," he said. He took out the driver's license and handed it to Antonio. "You want to remember your first one."

POOL FISHING

Barbara DeMarco-Barrett

The sun lumbered over the auto body shop across the street and a scrim of pink outlined its corrugated roof. The pool below my apartment turned my favorite color, sea glass, masking the murk that was all too apparent at high noon.

In my galley kitchen, I tipped Mr. Coffee over my cup and went out onto the landing. From my vantage point on the second floor of the Placent_a Arms—the "i" fizzled out long ago—apartment doors opened and dispelled men, mostly gardeners and construction workers. The still-fresh air smelled of salt from the ocean a mile away. When the Costa Mesa *fabricas*, auto body shops, and *taquerias* got busy, exhaust and fried food smells, not altogether unpleasant, replaced the salty fragrance.

The swimming pool drew my attention. On the surface of the water a Bud beer bottle bobbed about, not so unusual at the Arms, but the bottle looked stopped up with a plastic bag. Odd.

I retied the belt of my bathrobe and hurried down the prefab stone steps. The bottle was too far out to reach, but the leaf-sifter's pole was long; I used it to draw the bottle in. I hoped no one was watching. Silly, a grown woman circling forty, fishing bottles from a swimming pool. I returned the sifter to its place and tucked the trophy inside my robe, cold against my bare skin. The gravel-embedded laminate felt slick on the bottom of my feet as I rushed back upstairs.

My boyfriend Wyatt knew about my pool fishing obsession. He said I was the most unusual woman he knew. I had goldfish as pets and subscribed to *Fish World, Wrestling,* and *Popular Mechanics.* I stored my credit cards taped inside old magazines slumped in the rack, and my idea of a good time was volunteering at the soup kitchen up on 19th Street, not shopping. Please, no shopping. Online ordering worked just fine.

I used a pair of long tweezers to pull out the plastic bag, then set the bottle in the yellow shaft of light. A little slip of paper lay on the bottom. I dumped it out, along with a cigarette butt.

I didn't just rescue beer bottles. Beside my fifty-five-gallon fish tank, leaning in the corner, were a tricycle, an antique metal toaster, and a baseball bat.

I unfolded the little slip of paper with no expectation of what I would find. Prince Charming chain-smoking his worries away, wondering where I was?

A police helicopter groaned overhead, common in West Side Costa Mesa, known as Costa Misery to those of us biding our time here. I decided the smeary letters were an E and a P and another E. Moisture blurred the ink. I held the paper up to the light.

The words: Help me, came into focus. *Help me?*

It had to be a joke, designed by someone who knew I fished things out of the pool. Wyatt. He did it, just to get my goat. He got me good.

I left the bottle in the middle of the table, along with the slip of paper, and spent the day futzing around. Wyatt came over at six to fetch me for dinner—our weekly date at Wahoo's Fish Tacos. Big spender, my Wyatt. I observed his expression as his eyes landed on the bottle.

"Either you're drinking earlier and earlier," he said, "or

you've gone pool fishing again."

"Very funny," I said, and waited.

He waited, too. "What?"

"What do you mean what?"

"What!"

"You didn't do that?" I gestured at the bottle. "Stop playing with me already."

"I love playing with you," he said, pulling me close, running his finger under my tee-shirt and further north.

I told him about finding the bottle, but he was rubbing me up here and down there, the way I like it.

"You missed your calling," I said, although I didn't exactly know what I meant by that. I kicked the door shut and we stumbled across the hardwood floor to the sofa where Wyatt continued to do what he does best.

As we showered, soaping each other's backs and fronts and underneaths, I said, "Somebody's in trouble."

"One of your neighbors is playing with you." He soaped my arms. "A neighbor sees you fishing things out of the pool, gets bored, and thinks, who can I mess with? You, that's who."

"No," I said, rinsing off and stepping onto the red bath mat. I wrapped myself in a red bath sheet. "I can feel it. Something's wrong."

He turned off the water. I handed him the other bath sheet.

He followed me into the living room. Late day sun slotted in through the blinds. The pool shone below, all turquoisey and bright, as if we were at a lux Orange County resort and not a converted motel on the misery side of town.

"I can't just do nothing," I said.

"You're so dramatic," he said, coming up behind me.

The sky was the color of plums. Streetlights on Placentia, beyond the parking lot, flashed on. Three crows perched on the phone wires above the street.

"Look," I said. "Those same crows were there this morning in the identical same place."

"You sure?"

"I'm sure."

"Damn," he said, letting out a breath. Wyatt didn't believe in much, but he did believe in crow symbolism. Those muscular black birds didn't scare me—I thought they were beautiful—but they scared Wyatt, who was at least six-feet tall and had arms like river rocks from hefting all that furniture at work. But his fright happened on the inside, which his brawny self couldn't protect.

We went to Wahoo's and I scanned the menu. You'd think I'd have it memorized by now. I ordered fish tacos with guac on the side. Afterward, we went to Goat Hill Tavern and got drunk on martinis. Wyatt's good that way: Whichever way I'm headed, he's by my side.

We were both too drunk to drive, so we called an Uber and as the Prius pulled up to my not-so-fancy home sweet home, I squinted at the sign.

"You think anyone notices the burned out 'i'?" I said to Wyatt.

"What 'i'?" he said.

I looked up at the newly formed word, Placent_a, in old blue neon, which made me think of childbirth and how it might be the most surreal thing I would ever be lucky enough to experience. I had a smidgen of time left.

In the parking lot, the newest resident, a burly dude with long sideburns, in jeans and a denim vest, jumped from a four-by-four truck you needed a ladder to climb into. He hunched over as he carried a six-pack of Bud and a bouquet of supermarket flowers up the steps.

"Wyatt," I said, stumbling from the cab.

He paid the Uber driver and followed me to the stairs.

"Hmm?"

"That guy," I said, gesturing in Burly Dude's direction as he disappeared through an apartment door.

Wyatt's attention swerved to the opposite direction. On the corner adjacent to the Arms, cop car lights whirled about, a dizzying holiday. A shiny lowrider with yellow stripes flanking the metallic purple side idled by the curb. A cop had the Hispanic driver up against the car, frisking him. The West Side of Costa Misery segued from middle class to lower middle class and Hispanic, which meant Hispanics were the ones hassled by the police.

"This place is so racist," I said, moving in their direction, but Wyatt held me back.

"Down, girl," he said.

I stopped. I needed to stop reacting without thinking. It would get me into trouble someday.

Upstairs, the August heat of the apartment closed in, so we left our clothes in a puddle on the floor and jumped in the shower where we did more than bathe.

Wyatt left at sun-up, but not before he said, "Top of the morning to ya!" He drove a furniture truck for a factory up the 91 in the Inland Empire, which was more desolate than empire-like. I was thinking about Burly Dude with beer and flowers. I still had a bad feeling.

I poured more coffee and sat at the table. My apartment, situated in the center of the U, afforded me a view of apartments on both sides. Just when I thought nothing would happen, Burly Dude appeared through his door on the far end. He stomped down the steps, making my apartment vibrate, started his 4x4, and drove away.

I pulled on a pair of jeans and T-shirt, slipped into flipflops, and moseyed onto the landing. Already the heat was creeping upwards. I padded to Burly Dude's apartment and listened. Next door, Marta emerged, shouldering a tote bag with spray bottles.

"Hey, Marta," I said. "Do you know the guy who moved in there?"

She frowned. "You mean *couple*? He not so nice to his lady."

"What do you mean?"

"She cry. A lot. I sorry. I get to bus. Rich people need clean house." She tapped her tote brimming with cleaning fluids.

I returned to Burly Dude's door and pressed my ear against it. I heard the distinct sound of a morning TV show and what sounded like a human cough. I tried the doorknob, then knocked. Nothing. Knocked again. I heard what sounded like someone moaning, trying to call for help but having trouble getting the words out. I jiggled the knob. There was a little give.

I ran home for something to pick the lock. When my older brother was a kid, he taught me how to pick locks—preparation for his later life of crime, which moved him to his current happy home, Chino State Prison.

Back at the door, I stuck my crochet hook into the lock and miracle of miracles, the door opened. I gave a little push. An apartment layout just like mine—big rectangular living room, tiny kitchen. A vase with the flowers Burly Dude carried home last night. The bedroom door was closed. I went to it and listened. *Good Morning America.* It squeaked open. On a straight-back chair sat a young woman in a football jersey with the number 42. She was tied up, duct tape over her mouth. Her dark eyes were as big and round as malted milk balls.

I went to her and peeled back the duct tape.

"He's coming right back," she said. "Went out for food."

"Why'd he tie you up?"

"Tried to break up with him. You should go."

A pink comforter covered the bed. A clock radio sat on the nightstand. Framed photos on the dresser.

"Does he always keep you tied up in here?"

"Just when he goes out."

"I'll be back," I said, and pressed the duct tape back onto her face.

As I eased out of the room, the truck pulled in. I locked and closed the door to the apartment. I was at the top of the stairway by my place when Burly Dude reached the top. My heart was going to explode out of my chest any second.

He smiled but his eyes held no light. A heart tatt decorated his muscly forearm and he carried a Del Taco bag. "Morning," he said.

"Morning."

I rushed into my apartment and watched through the Venetian blinds as he unlocked the door. He noticed something was different, but not different enough to stop him. Crows sat on the phone lines. I had to do something, but what?

I called the police and told my story to the dispatcher, who said she'd send someone over when an officer freed up.

"What part of 'woman tied up in a chair' don't you get? How long am I supposed to wait?"

"We'll have someone there just as soon as we can," she said, her voice tired, jaded.

"I swear," I said, and tried calling Wyatt but got his voice mail.

My heart wouldn't slow down. I broke a sweat—from the heat of the day or my upset, maybe both.

I scanned the apartment for something I could use for protection, if necessary. A dumbbell was the only thing I owned that could do serious damage. Gurgling from the tank drew my attention. The air filter had come loose again. I tightened it as Wanda and the other fish skimmed the top of the tank looking for food. As I replaced the lid, I saw it, the baseball bat. Better than a dumbbell. Easier to swing.

I sat and paced, sat and paced, all the while keeping a watch on Burly Dude's apartment. Doors opened and Hispanic women and children poured out—going to their cleaning jobs, walking kids to school. Finally, Burly Dude's door opened. He got back into his truck and it growled away. I took the crochet hook and baseball bat that leaned in the corner, and hurried to the apartment, all the while praying to St. George, the saint of courage and bravery, that I would rescue the woman before I shorted out from a case of nerves.

I picked the lock and was in the apartment before anyone else left their apartment. When I opened the bedroom door, the woman's wide eyes said, Get me the hell out of here. I peeled back the duct tape.

"Thank God," she said.

"Where'd your boyfriend go?"

"Ex-boyfriend," she said. "He's a process server, had papers to serve."

I undid the knots.

"He's a nice guy," she said, "except when he's mad. He was always throwing beer bottles into the pool. You were always fishing them out and I had to try."

I undid the last knot. "How long have you been in this chair?"

She got up, kicked out her limbs, and ran into the bathroom. "Days!" she called. Then she was in the kitchen, downing a tall glass of water. Her arms wore purple splotches.

"He do that to you?"

"He was upset I was leaving."

I felt my face grow red. "We should go," I said, throwing the baseball bat over my shoulder. "You have someone you can stay with?"

She was taking her time in the kitchen. Maybe she didn't want to leave. Women could be like that, not want to be set free. I stood watch at the front door. She ran to the bedroom and bathroom and was still throwing things into a bag when the truck roared into the lot.

"He's back," I said.

She joined me, an unzipped backpack hanging from one hand. She chewed the fingernails of her other hand.

He was out of the truck and on his way.

"C'mon." I pulled her along, having no idea what we were going to do when we saw him.

We were out on the landing when he hit the bottom step. He was busy watching his feet when he looked up.

"What the fuck?" he said.

He picked up his pace. He was on the landing before us.

"Natalie," he said.

When he grabbed at her arm, I held the bat as if I were about to swing at a ball.

"Hey," I said.

"I swear, Nat, I'm gonna kick your ass over this," he said.

Natalie began crying.

"Take the back stairs," I said, jabbing the air with my index finger. "Now."

Burly Dude and I faced off. He grabbed at the bat, but I've always been fast on my feet, and when I'm pissed off, there's no stopping me. I jumped back in time. He grasped at air.

"Guys like you ruin it for the good ones," I said, letting the statement hang in the air between us. I backed up into the far corner, out of the line of sight of the office. He came at me. I swung at his knees and he fell. He pulled himself up and I thought of Natalie's bruises and of my best friend's sister in Alabama whose husband strangled her, wrapped her up in plastic, and buried her in the woods behind their house.

Who else would Burly Dude hurt if I didn't do something?

"Bitch," he said, and that's when I saw stars. Name-calling must trigger something in me because my vision shattered into gray and white shimmering splotches. I swung the bat against his skull, hard. He looked surprised. I pushed at his torso as hard as I could with the tip of the bat, and when that wasn't enough, I dropped the bat and used my hands. He grabbed onto the railing but lost his footing and flipped over. His skull bounced against the bullnose edge of the pool.

Down below, Natalie screamed and scampered out of the office, followed by the manager. They bent over him. I joined them, and soon the EMTs and police were everywhere.

They agreed it had been an awful accident, and after I spent the day at the police station, they released me. Wyatt was waiting, still in his work clothes, hands deep in his pockets.

"What the hell, Mimi?"

"I had to help a neighbor."

"You must've done more than help a neighbor for them to bring you here."

"The guy with the Bud and the flowers. He fell from the landing, and I was a witness, so they brought me in."

"Accidentally fell?"

"He threatened his girlfriend, then he threatened me. He lost his footing and fell. That's it."

We hurried from the Costa Misery police station to the car across the street. Wyatt's mouth fastened into a frown.

"He was a rat," I said.

Wyatt beeped the remote to unlock his Tundra. He opened the passenger's door and I climbed in.

"He was holding his girlfriend hostage," I said. "I had to do something."

He breathed out hard and gave me a sidelong glance. I would never tell Wyatt or anyone what had really happened. I couldn't. The world was better off with one less rat. I would soothe myself with that thought, which at first would be often, and then, not so much.

BREATH

Cheryl Garrett

They came in a cop car to get me. I was ready. I had on my combat boots, with the pink laces, the only combat boots I had left. I had changed from my skirt and blouse to jeans and a tight T-shirt. I didn't need any extra material between me and my rifle. Freddie told me I would get a bulletproof vest. When I walked out of my house with my rifle in its wooden crate, one of the cops jumped out of the car to take it. I pushed him away. I am the only one who touches the crate. I put it in the backseat, on the cushion next to me. The driver said nothing, and the three of us drove away.

Breathe, I told myself. Breathe. Out the window, I could see where the hot Texas sun had burned the trees that lined my block. If we were lucky, we would be there in fifteen minutes. If we weren't lucky…I just couldn't think about that. The backseat smelled of tobacco and booze. Some worse odor lingered on the seats and rose up when I rearranged my butt.

Darlene was still in school. She would be fine. I had called Mother to pick her up, or Carol could, and then let the girls play together. Mother would soon figure out where I was. I heard a sharp crackle from the car radio. I tried not to hear the words. Breathe.

The driver cop slightly turned to me, telling me my vest was in the trunk. I nodded. The two cops then looked ahead, concentrating on the road as we hurriedly skirted the traffic. We weren't using sirens yet. I watched the landscape out the window change from neighborhoods to city streets and tall buildings. We were getting closer.

Dad taught me how to shoot an old .22 bore when I was six or seven. It was small though not quite small enough, and sometimes I had bruises. I got good at shooting when we were at our lake cabin, beating Janie and Jeff, who were three years older. I could shoot all five coffee cans off the log with only five bullets.

When I was ten, Dad put the big shotgun in my arms, pointed it to the hay pile and said, "shoot." I pushed the butt of the shotgun against the small of my shoulder and fired. The blast blew me backward, and I fell hard on my butt. My shoulder hurt for days and stayed black and blue longer. Mother was pissed about the shotgun. I heard them fighting late into the night.

"I don't care if it's a ten-gauge or two-gauge, she doesn't need to shoot a shotgun at her age," Mother yelled.

"Two-gauge." I smiled to myself as we kept driving.

I heard the sirens then. An ambulance zoomed past, and I opened the crate. The rifle was in three parts and was immaculate. I cleaned it every Sunday though I hadn't used it for two or three weeks. I began the assembly, careful not to bump it in the close backseat. The rifle had been a gift from Michael's Gun Shop, advertising of sorts. It was a reward for my last winnings, the 1965 Texas Turkey Shoot. They had offered me a Winchester, all the trimmings on the gun, but I wanted the German Anchütz. All I needed was a good scope and a clean, well-weighted barrel. I loved this rifle.

Breathe. We stopped about three blocks from the outskirts

of campus. That seemed the closest we could get since other cop cars were everywhere, blocking the streets, up on sidewalks, abandoned. The car radio squawked again. I heard the chaos as I opened my door. Pop, pop and screams colliding with the wind. My God. I froze. I don't shoot living things. I turned to the cop in the front seat, the other now opening my door. I never hunted, much to my Dad's dismay. I looked at the two cops. They were waiting for me to get out of the car.

"Miss, we need you. If you're as good as they say, we need you."

I heard another scream and saw a few people run from a campus building to a store on the other side of the street. Shit. I got out, carrying the rifle, but the scope was still in my hand. I took the vest from the cop, and awkwardly put it on. I had never worn one of these things. I finished locking the scope into place and checked the trigger. Another cop came running toward us from the campus area, telling us to keep our heads low. A small plane flew overhead, much too close to be safe. I heard more pops.

Breathe. We walked a block closer, trying to get to the center of campus. At first, I didn't realize there was a body on the ground. I thought it was a tree trunk, lying on the grass. I stumbled, and a cop grabbed my elbow.

"Don't look," he said.

Then Freddie was there, thank god. "Where have you been?" his first words were scolding.

"I was hurrying. You know, I had to go home first. For this." I held the rifle up slightly. He handed me a box of ammunition. "The good stuff," he assured me. I looked at the label and then opened the box to check. Yep, slick, brass, and greased. The $30-a-box bullets. I stuck the box in my vest pocket. The vest was too big and incredibly hot. I couldn't fire with it on. Once in the building I would have to take it off, I told Freddie.

He nodded. "Let's go. Stick close to that building over

there and run when you can. The other guys and I are going to go over by the short wall and distract him. You're to get to the tower. That's where he's holed up. Stay to the periphery. Stay behind something, anything." He looked worried. I smiled to show I understood.

I knew the campus. The first year I was here, I ended up in the riflery class for my P.E. credit. I figured the class would be an easy A. The coach spotted me immediately, the way I held the gun, the steadiness of my stance and, best of all, the way I took directions. Our four-man, one-woman team won the district that year, me being the only woman on any team. The next year we won sectionals, with three women on our team. We put pink shoelaces in our combat boots, stuck our swinging ponytails in caps and smiled broadly when we entered the range. By my senior year, we won nationals.

I took a step toward the closest building, trying to stoop. A shot popped beside me, skittering the dirt on my boot. Another pop. I froze.

I stood mesmerized, watching the horror, as three or four people ran past me, one was bloody, holding his arm, his face full of fear. "Don't look," I told myself. "Breathe." The screams were now on all sides of me, and another pop-pop of a rifle split the hot air.

Freddie yelled, "Go," breaking my shock, and we all took off in three different directions. He and the other guys ran toward the center, yelling at one another. I followed the hedge, all of us hoping for the tower. I had to stop by the time I had run a block. I was hot in the vest, and the rifle weighed too much. I hung back behind a one-story bicycle shack, trying to decide on where to go next. I looked up to see a small line of smoke from the top of the tower. The sniper was up there. Oh hell. Up, the perfect place for any shooter to... Breathe.

Pop, another too close to me. Then a scream from a man only thirty feet away. I started to run again. First, to my left, close to a tree and another short building. Concentrate. Then to the next building, closing in on the tower, using trees as cover, hoping for shadow, but it was nearly noon. I had to stop, sitting down, hugging the back of a stucco brick dorm. Breathe.

I saw Freddie wave to someone, wave for them to stay. He knelt by a stone bench, then looked around. He was looking for me. I waved, and he shook his head "no." No waving I decided. Draws attention. I tore through the hedge next to me and got behind a nearby low temporary.

Freddie and I had met at a South Texas Shoot-out. I had been the first woman to beat him at anything, and he took it badly. The next rifle meet, he was ready for me, jeering and teasing, talking about my skinny ass and long ponytail. I beat him so badly that day, I thought I saw a tear in his eye. I wanted that win. He shouldn't have teased me. That time he took it well. He bought me a beer and apologized. We try to get together, but my kid and his school. Breathe. Concentrate.

I army-crawled along the backside of the building, inching ever closer to the tower. Pop, pop. Three more screams. I saw a young woman go down. These people were dying. He was killing all these people. Breathe, concentrate.

I ran from the cover of the building to the hedge. Two cops were firing at the top of the tower from the back of a group of trees. Those were impossible shots. Too far and bad trajectory. The sniper was behind some sort of brick wall that surrounded the tower balcony. Nobody could shoot him from down here.

This close to the tower, the scene turned more gruesome. Seven or eight people were either lying on the sidewalk or grass. Twenty or so were running anywhere to get out of range. Pop, pop. I ran to the right side of the tower as the cops let out a stream of bullets. I stopped at the entrance under the porch, not knowing where to go. Breathe.

A cop yelled from behind me. "Here, here." He must have noticed my rifle and my vest. "We can get in over here." I crawled to the side door of the tower.

"Miss Anderson? Oh, thank the lord, you're here." The cop smiled slightly. The one next to him just stared, saying little. I was used to this. In Texas it wasn't unusual to see a woman with a gun, but a woman sharpshooter was a different story.

Freddie jumped into the large foyer suddenly. "Get her up there. We need to find some way to get her a line of sight."

The two guys with Freddie had some kind of military uniforms, complete with large rifles and bigger scopes. They led four of us to the elevators.

One said, "He's on the twenty-eighth floor, the Observation Deck. We'll stop at the twenty-seventh and see what the area looks like from a floor below. See if we can lock onto him."

I nodded and looked at Freddie. He nodded, barely. His uniform was sweaty, his hair on ends. He had this habit of running his hands through his large mop of hair when he was stressed. Today, he'd left his cowboy hat, and his hair was standing nearly straight up. I had an urge to push it down into place. A mother's urge. Darlene. Breathe.

I leaned against the elevator wall, waiting for the military guys to scope out the twenty-seventh floor and stairway.

At twelve, I had gone with my dad on my first hunting trip. I would never go again. It had been a beautiful crisp, November morning, the first day of deer season. We were at the lake house, walking through the wet grass, dew sparkling in the early sunrise. I was excited, scared, hungry. In the deer blind, we quietly waited for the first buck to come to the salt lick. Dad got the first shot.

"Shoot to kill," he had warned me. "We don't want an injured deer dragging around. That's cruel." The hunter's code. We got out of the blind to see Dad's perfect shot. I looked at the deer and left for the car. I didn't get out until we were home.

The cops returned on the elevator with the two other guys and Freddie. "Let's take her to the window on the twenty-seventh. The one right below the deck. See what she thinks," Freddie said.

The ride up was slow. Freddie got out first, motioning us to follow. "Here," Freddie called, and we all moved over to the window directly under the sniper. "Can you lean out?"

He looked at me, covered in vest, tree leaves, dirt and sweat. I handed Freddie the rifle and leaned out the window.

"I can lean out, but not with the gun. It's too heavy." He agreed. We went back to the elevator.

When we got to the twenty-eighth floor, the cops again walked around, quickly opening doors, looking out windows. I stood in the middle, holding my rifle, waiting for instructions. The pops were even louder up here, but the screams were fainter.

Suddenly, the elevator bell rang, and another man, one in a dark suit, stepped out. We all stared at him, I with the rifle on my shoulder and other cops with guns drawn.

"Special Agent Walker, FBI," he said quickly, flipping open his lapel to show a badge.

I hate the FBI. One afternoon, when I was in college, I was practicing at the range when a man dressed like this guy walked over to me. He never introduced himself. Instead, while I'm gearing up, focusing, breathing, he stated, "FBI, we need to see you over in the office." In Texas, a person asks, but this was an order. I wasn't in the Army. I don't like taking orders. He pointed his chin to the little corner of the range, an enclosed closet with windows. I turned around and continued to work with the rifle.

"Miss," he said louder, assuming I didn't hear clearly. "You need to step over to the office, now." I didn't move. He reached down and grabbed my arm, my rifle clattered to the floor.

My coach yelled from the back, "Hold on, hold on." Within three seconds my coach was there. "Rachel, please, just do as he says. It's really no big deal." By now everyone in the range, all twenty or so cadets, sat down, fascinated.

"Okay." I got up, checking my rifle and the scope.

"No, leave the gun here," the FBI guy ordered. I looked at coach and he nodded. "Miss Anderson, you are being ordered to give the FBI your fingerprints. It is the requirement for any citizen who reaches sharpshooter status to have his fingerprints taken."

Coach stepped in. "You gotta practice. Nationals are coming up."

I yielded. The FBI got my fingerprints and the NRA sent me a life membership, free of charge, that same week. I tore it up. I don't shoot living things.

"What we need to do here is get a line of sight." Walker stated as if he were taking over. Pop, pop. Another scream.

"There is no line of sight from this floor, either," Freddie stated. "We have to go up to the observation deck."

Walker agreed. "We've got to get him before he kills more people down there." Pop, pop. Breathe, breathe.

"We have to go up. Break open the door to the deck some

way," one of the cops pleaded.

We heard the plane overhead. Freddie turned to the cop, "Go outside and radio the plane. Tell them to start shooting in ten minutes. Give us cover." The cop nodded and ran to the elevator. Freddie turned to me. "We're going up."

The stairs were under the exit sign, two flights to a closed door, the deck door. Breathe.

I walked last, holding my rifle pointed to the ground. I took the ammo box out of the vest and squeezed it into my jeans' pocket. On the landing, I dropped the vest. The FBI guy looked at me twice.

"Who's she?" he asked as we quickly walked up the next flight.

"Our sniper," Freddie stated flatly. He wanted no questions. He went back down the stairs and discussed our situation, in a rather determined whisper. I ignored them. I concentrated on my breathing.

Freddie walked ahead of me and then slowly twisted the knob of the door leading to the deck. The sniper hadn't locked the door, thank god. Pop, pop, pop. How much ammunition did this guy have? The cops had said one shooter; I had to hope they were right. We had eight minutes before the plane started its cover.

Freddie opened the door two inches immediately after the next pop and peered out. He closed it without a sound and turned to me.

"The guy's got a casket of ammunition and a bunch of guns on the concrete beside him. It's only one man. Can you sight him through the crack when the door is open?"

I nodded, confused.

"The door is jammed some way. He's got something against it, hoping that keeps it closed. All we got is about a five-inch passage," Freddie explained, keeping it brief.

Breathe, concentrate. "Okay. That's what we got. Give me thirty seconds to sight and then..." I looked away.

"Once. You fire once," Freddie confirmed, "and then you run down those stairs. Everyone else step away from the door and go down the stairs. If she misses, he'll be coming for us, so be prepared to shoot."

One of the cops looked nervously at Freddie. "Is she that good?" There was no reply. I looked at the guys on the stairs. Their sweating faces, raw nerves showing signs of outright terror.

Freddie looked down at me, a few steps below. "Rachel," he was grinning. "I hate to admit that you're better than me." I stared at the door. "It's just another day at the range," he promised. "And, Rachel, remember. This is my shot. You were never here."

I nodded.

Sweat was forming again, over my eyes, under my arms. Freddie took my rifle, checked it over and handed it back, smiling his approval. I took the ammo box out of my pocket, opening and sliding out the long, thin bullet. The bullet was greased slick so it would slide easily through the chamber. No wiggles. I walked up to the step just below the door.

At the door, I pushed the bullet into the chamber and slid the bolt closed.

Breathe, breathe.

I learned how to breathe from my coach. He said that breathing at the right time would really improve my shooting, but I didn't realize how much a difference it made. I learned to listen to my breath, to control my heartbeat, to slow my body down to a final exhale.

"All right." The men had moved down the stairs, watching and listening. Freddie stood by the door, ready to open it. Pop, pop, sirens and yelling, screaming, pleading. Concentrate.

I knelt as close to the door as I could and still give it room to open. I steadied my body, put the rifle up to my shoulder, finding the sweet spot, and leaned over the sight. Freddie put his hand on the knob, then twisted. We waited. Breathe.

And then the plane came over, with more pops. Pops from the deck and from the plane. Freddie inched the door open, I lowered the rifle, breathing two, three times. Then the door was open enough for me to see him, hunched over his own rifle, ignoring the bullets hailing down from the plane.

Breathe in, then out. My riflescope was on his heart. A human heart.

There is just the right second when the breath leaves the body, when the air is out, that the body is in stasis. No movement, no blinking, just still.

A DISCREET PERSONAL ASSISTANT

Jo Perry

1.

No loose ends—that is everything.

Nothing before or after to indicate anything out of the ordinary—no ripples disrupting the blind, smooth surface of the everyday.

No noise.

No embarrassing entreaties. No confessions. No messes.

Everything must remain precise and businesslike. Respectful, but impersonal.

It's not the *what* that matters in the end, for God's sake. Everyone—the brave, the stupid, the fortunate, the malicious, the innocent—if there are such people—and the guilty will arrive at the "what."

"What" is a destination, that's all. A cliché.

What is a place that's always been there, that you don't see until the very end when it is suddenly obvious and in your face—a mirroring otherworld like the negative space in an Escher print.

What is a metal door slamming on a windowless, black,

vertical, box-shaped room. It's the settling in and the rattle of the locks turning, then clicking shut.

It's dark air gulped fast.

What is a whole-body panic igniting a cosmic light show inside the skull.

What is two still darknesses becoming one. What is a vertiginous slip and then the fall after the ingestion of a foreign substance. What is the present bleeding out into the past.

What is everything.

But the *what* is not the point at all.

2.

You get what you pay for and I only accept PayPal.

My customers are sophisticated and discerning. If a simple murder is what you want, go elsewhere.

Think of me as a first-class travel agent for souls. A coach. A tour guide. A coyote.

A discreet personal assistant.

A reverse midwife. An event planner—a planet declutterer.

An executor, an expediter—not an executioner. Or an escort.

You choose.

Nothing irritates me more than a slobbering post-midlife-crisis thick-gutted lawyer or doctor or banker—weeping that he spent his retirement fund, savings and investments on prostitutes and strippers, and who needs a life insurance payout for his children's college tuitions and to subsidize the lifestyle that his soon-to-be widow will require—begging me to murder him.

Good luck with your crap life and your crap death, Sir—I'm a facilitator, not a marriage counselor.

I arrange transfers.

A destroyer of worlds does not operate a clean-up service for fools, for God's sake.

I don't do death—I am death.

3.

Obviously, my unique business model cannot rely on referrals.

My clients locate me the way rivers find the sea—unseen and mighty forces shift them toward me.

Fear. Dread. Certainty. Ennui. Crushing solitude.

And sometimes serendipity—like the story in last week's *Post* about the burgeoning number of services that remove the human stains, maggots and debris that the 30,000-plus people who die alone every year in Japan leave behind as their legacies.

Or the existential itch that develops suddenly in the oncologist's waiting room while reading a science magazine article about the alarming number of dogs who eat their deceased masters.

It creeps, but the time always arrives when what one needs is neither a lover nor a friend, but a judicious and confidential personal assistant to tie up loose ends, to purge, to simplify, to expedite and then to haul your carcass to the next level.

As you can imagine, accomplishing all of the above—and customizing the experience down to the most grotesquely minuscule detail—choosing the china pattern for the last course, or deciding whether the postprandial cup of tea should be caffeinated, green or black, with lemon, sugar or honey, cream or milk—is an enormous, complex, and perilous undertaking.

Thus, the compensation I require is steep and unrefundable, and I am choosy about the clients whom I consent to serve.

I am preparing to review an applicant right now.

His or her oblique yet eager email inquiry in response to my cryptic advertisement in the Personals seems mildly promising:

Dear Sir or Madam,

I urgently seek an experienced professional to assist me in arranging an extremely important journey in the near future.

I look forward to hearing from you as soon as possible regarding my inquiry.

Yours Sincerely,
A.E. Darling

Pretty damn perfect, wouldn't you say?

And Darling is desperate, which is always immensely helpful.

And A.E. Darling may be a bit too perfect. The inquiry could be a trap.

But that would be impossible. And the smooth and eager Mr. or Ms. Darling has miles to go before I will even deign to consider him or her as client. I know too much and have arranged too many journeys to be disarmed.

I'm ice too frigid to thaw, too hard to con.

And yes, I replied to A.E. Darling's inquiry—but not immediately. It's always useful to dump a mountain of busy work on the desperate and then to make them wait. In reply to his inquiry, A.E. Darling received a twenty-page confidential application, detailed financial and medical history forms, a nondisclosure agreement that requires a notary, and a hefty PayPal invoice.

I'll admit I was surprised when after just three hours the completed applications and statements were returned as tidy PDF attachments to another positively courtly, and still eager email, along with confirmation that the money had been transferred to one of my numerous accounts.

I merely skimmed the forms.

A.E. Darling's swift and deferential fulfillment of all that I required resulted in a month-long silence from me and then a laconic email informing him of his/her after-hours appointment at a tattoo shop run inside a failing muffler repair business in Vernon, an industrial area four miles south of downtown Los Angeles. The owner speaks Spanish and the operation is cash only. The faded sample designs stapled to the wall's bare beams—when they don't display realistic variations on Christ's crucifixion—are riffs on the Honduran flag.

I loiter—dressed in black and with a black balaclava covering my face and head—among rusted cars and piles of their broken anatomies in the gloom just beyond the building's shadow. A single anti-insect bulb illuminates the shop's entrance.

Then a car door thuds shut, the loose gravel grumbles a few times beneath a human foot, and the prospective client materializes.

Not another widow. Good. I'm up to my ass in bereaved women and could use a change of pace.

The would-be client is a slender, gray-haired man, winged scapulae visible under in a stylish and expensive camel-hair overcoat unusual for Southern California. As he steps toward the jumbled interior, the bug light turns his blue eyes a chemical green and sallows his pale skin and hair.

I move soundlessly around the building to a freshly Windexed, slightly open window as per the arrangement I made earlier with the proprietor and for which—along with a few other services—he received three thousand dollars.

I position myself to the left of the pane, where I can see the interior but am invisible to those inside.

A.E. Darling tilts his head and speaks inaudibly with the proprietor, who, as instructed, hands him a printed note:

Dear Sir or Madam,

If you are receiving this, you have followed instructions, honored all prohibitions outlined in our previous communication, and have arrived at the specified location on time and alone.

Thank you.

Punctuality will be necessary if you are to enjoy the services you seek. And if our business relationship is indeed formalized, know that more challenging, exacting—even disorienting—experiences await.

One rule must govern all future interactions: Do not ask questions.

There shall be no queries about why this thing and not

another, why here and not there, etc.

If after reading this you still wish to proceed, please review the enclosed design and initial this document where indicated to signify your approval and to certify that you ate a meal no less than four hours ago, are fully hydrated, have not taken blood-thinners, aspirin or NSAIDs during the prior forty-eight hours.

Please note that your initial is your commitment to comply exactly and completely with all post-tattoo application instructions.

Please do not email us.

You will be notified within thirty days if you have been approved. If you do not hear from us, your client application will have been denied.

Thank you for your interest and good luck.

A prospective client's response to the tattoo measures his docility, his hopelessness, his tolerance for pain, his capacity for passivity and his ability to remain silent—but the stinging body-alteration accomplishes more than that. It demonstrates that all instructions must be obeyed and that our little arrangement will require suffering and humiliation.

No pain, no gain, right?

But most of all, the tattoo signifies that the prospective client—although he does not comprehend the real meaning of the transaction to which he has consented—no longer belongs to himself.

The client is mine now.

4.

Dear Mr. A.E. Darling,

After a thorough review of your application and personal documents, we would like to welcome you as our newest client.

Receipt of this email signifies the commencement of the one-year period during which the contracted services will be provided to you in full without prior notification, i.e., without warning.

This email address will be deactivated immediately: Henceforth no alteration of or revocation of the vendor/client agreement will be permissible or possible.

There is no need to prepare for your journey in any way: We will take care of every detail.

Please know we will be working behind the scenes to create a stunning, utterly private, totally customized and effectively "natural" experience especially for you.

Relax and Seize the Day!

During the interval between that email and today, I've been busy with a number of taxing, yet satisfying dead-end client relationships that involved salt water and dehydration, a homemade untraceable nerve agent, fire, ice, a lethal hairy moth, toothpaste, and as a finale for all of the above, Las Vegas magician-worthy disappearances.

Poof.

No messes. No loose ends. No anything.

God, I'm exhausted. But A.E. Darling's contractual year has almost expired.

As I explained before, forcing the desperate to wait makes their unbearable anxiety piquant.

Still, each client's temperament, circumstances, and catastrophe are peculiar to him. Thus, the resolution I devise for A.E. Darling will be one-of-a-kind. Sure, I could recycle one of my greatest hits, but no reputable top-tier travel agent books his clients on the same one-way cruise to the same uninhabited island or arranges for all to be dropped into the same dark, impassable wilderness.

How dull would the world be if all travelers began their

journeys at the same time every year and their journeys were the same?

I am proud of my unwavering remoteness and my disciplined professionalism, but A.E. Darling's mute surrender to the excruciating and finalizing sternum tattoo entitles him to a novel—even whimsical—transition.

A review of my favorite client's medical history reveals only mild emphysema, hypertension controlled by medication, pronated feet, and spinal arthritis.

A.E. Darling didn't decide to go away because he's sick.

No, something else is pushing him out the door.

But I'm not interested in what led him to me—despair, failure, loneliness, criminality, sexual depravity, revenge or guilt—it doesn't matter.

Color me not curious. Ever.

I don't deal with hypotheticals. My focus is the practical, and the word "emphysema" on the medical form winked at me.

Thus, I found myself purchasing a run-down commercial building with a small basement below the corner space—incredibly rare in Los Angeles—near the tattoo place, but not too close. The deep, rectangular basement merely required soundproofing and waterproofing, installation of an interior security and video system, lighting, electrical upgrades and rewiring.

The building is a good very long-term investment and I'm in no hurry. It's a sullied beige, a mostly moribund, squat one-story block with three empty commercial spaces, a printing operation that's always closed, a morning-only doughnut/boba shop, and a filthy liquor store that looks like a jail for wine and spirits.

I spent a huge chunk of time observing—no studying—my client.

I was the frail, stooped old woman pushing her walker past A.E. Darling as he daily marked the sun's slow dive into the Pacific from the same bench in the same park in Santa

Monica, the *Los Angeles Times* folded neatly on his lap.

I was the heavy, bearded man in line behind A.E. Darling who waited to deposit his pension and investment checks at the bank in Pasadena. Did I mention that A.E. Darling is a retired engineer? Not that it matters, except that his work in the public and private sectors provided generous retirement packages.

I was also the teenager responsible for a series of early morning auto break-ins and thefts in A.E. Darling's neighborhood.

I was the new gardener working the leaf blower at the new house across the street from A.E. Darling's small, trim Spanish bungalow in Silverlake.

I was the middle-aged woman in thick, red-framed glasses reading a bodice-ripper while dining alone in the back booth of the restaurant where A.E. Darling consumes his evening meals. He's a vegetarian with an almost childish sweet tooth—chocolate cream pie, and ice cream sundaes with extra cherries on top are his favorites—and works on the *New York Times* crossword puzzle as he eats.

I have become a shadowy silhouette inside his shadow. That hazy shape just beyond the periphery. The not-sound, not-silence audible between clock ticks. The hush right before dawn that might be a stranger's quiet breathing.

If A.E. Darling has buddies or family, girlfriends or boyfriends, they're not visible. But an examination of his mail revealed a John Darling in Delaware, Vivian Darling Gates in Buffalo, New York, and what looked like a greeting card— lime green Hallmark envelope addressed in sloping script—likely a birthday greeting from a work pal who retired to Arizona.

I've learned that clients often choose to travel on the anniversary of their births, but not this one. A.E. Darling's birthday came and went with no change of routine. Darling's a bit different. More self-contained than most—and despite what must be his growing desperation as his year runs out—always aloof.

I, too, am aloof. Always in control. But as the moment

when I can finally serve my client approaches, I must confess that I'm excited—and impressed as always with my own inventiveness, cleverness and professionalism. He will never appreciate it, of course, but what I have created for A.E. Darling is a masterpiece.

It is four a.m., three days before A.E. Darling's three hundredth and sixty-fifth contractual day. Weary from anxiety and from waiting for whatever he has coming, my client has descended into a troubled, Ambien-induced sleep.

His breathing is irregular and the muscles in his hands twitch slightly—like a dog who is dream-chasing squirrels. I chose extended-release zolpidem tartrate (Ambien) delivered in a *chocolat pot au crème* instead of via a hanky infused with a volatile agent like diethyl ether or chloroform. A.E. Darling has a prescription bottle of Ambien in his bathroom cupboard, so any trace discovered in a toxicology screening—and believe me, the way I've arranged things, there won't be a screening or a post-mortem—would be unremarkable. And I'm fond of zolpidem tartrate for older clients because of its tendency to cause disorientation and dizziness, and to produce hallucinations.

I promised a wild ride—an adventure—and my client shall have just that from the first to the last moment—with the exception of the sedate just-below-the-speed-limit, thirty-minute drive from his residence to the building housing the basement refuge I carefully outfitted and prepared.

Even under the influence, A.E. Darling remains silent and deferential. I half-push, half-lead him into the indirectly and softly illuminated soundproof basement; then, when his hands shake too hard to unclasp the buttons, I remove the top of his sky-blue pajamas.

The tattoo has healed nicely: "DO NOT RESUSCITATE" marches across the pale skin of his almost hairless barrel chest like a banner.

My client squints, then widens his lapis lazuli eyes to gaze at the oxygen tanks arranged with balletic precision, and upon the shining, humming chamber waiting just for him.

Only the top of the line will do for A.E. Darling. Only a quiet, dignified undetectable and natural departure under the curved Plexiglas hood designed for maximum comfort and to prevent claustrophobia.

And what could be more natural than too much of a life-giving and beautiful substance—pure oxygen?

Aren't I clever?

I always loathe this part, but my clients always expect it. "Anything you'd like to say? To tell me before we begin?"

A.E. Darling blinks as though he has just awakened, then says in a tinny voice, "I am an ordinary man. Selfish and dull and worthless. I will not be missed. And I am sick to death of being trapped inside my own skin and my own head."

I wait a moment to acknowledge his declaration, grateful that he says nothing more.

I take A.E. Darling's trembling hand and escort him the few steps to the open hatch at the foot of the hyperbaric chamber the way a bride leads her groom to the marriage bed. "Let's get you settled in," I say. "Would you like music? I have classical, pop, rock and folk and easy listening. The lights dimmed or brightened? And would you like anything to drink?"

My client speaks his last words, "No, thank you," then bows toward the open hatch.

"Wait," he says suddenly and turns his fear-blanched face to me. "And after? There can be no fuss. No scandal."

As if your family in Buffalo or wherever cares, I think. "No worries, Mr. Darling. No fuss, no scandal is my forte. Your grieving family and friends will be consoled by the knowledge that you died peacefully of natural causes in your sleep. And you will, sir. I promise."

A.E. Darling nods, then crawls along the seven-hundred-and-fifty-thread-count Pima cotton sheet—static causing his fine gray hairs to rise for a moment—then reaches the ergonomic pillow I provided for his comfort.

My client folds his arms across his tattooed chest, closes his weird blue eyes to the world and sighs.

I secure the hatch, set the pressure to 1.6ATA and double-check the oxygen. Perfect. The pure oxygen will cause tinnitus, muscle spasms, convulsions, unconsciousness and, finally, worse—most of which my sedated, then insensate client will not feel.

Twelve boring—for me—minutes elapse. A.E. Darling rubs his mouth, blinks, then pounds the Plexiglas.

I pick up the phone connected to the chamber's interior and mask my annoyance. "Yes, sir?"

"I'm sorry, but I'm terribly thirsty and would love some water. Is that drink you offered still available?"

"Of course."

I step away from the chamber controls and remove a bottle of water from the refrigerator I've stocked with wine and beer and a few sweets, just in case.

I work the console and open the latch, then crawl into the oxygenated chamber, pulling the hatch closed to keep the oxygen level high.

I purchased the finest, most secure and roomiest chamber available to maximize my client's transitional experience. It's perfect. There's room inside for me to slither along the sheet covering to A.E. Darling's thin form. Halfway in, I extend the chilled bottle toward him and a spark leaps from the finely threaded cotton.

The thirsting, doomed A.E. Darling leans toward me to receive the drink when a clicking, sparking, then roaring fire-cloud confuses and inhabits the sealed, shatterproof chamber's interior, the pure oxygen's constant flow and my writhing client's screams enlivening the flames.

My face and body ablaze, I struggle to open the hatch with burning hands—but the hatch rim has fused shut.

How can this be possible?

Can this agony be real?
I don't do death, I am death.
Destroyer of worlds.
Everything is perfect.
No messes.
No loose ends.

LIKE DÉJÀ VU ALL OVER AGAIN

Melinda Loomis

This part of the park is quiet, shady, and secluded. My ancient Toyota Corolla sits at the edge of a shallow ravine. A silver guardian angel charm and a four-inch-long canister of pepper spray dangle from the keychain hanging from the car's ignition.

Both front windows are rolled down, allowing for a pleasant breeze. I sit in the passenger seat because it gives me more room to stretch out. The seat is all the way back and my feet are tucked up on the dash, and I'm busily writing in my journal. Hopes, dreams, to-do lists...important things that I swear I'm going to get to one of these days.

A clean-cut man appears out of nowhere. He calmly opens the driver's side door and slides into my car like he owns it.

"Hey, what are you—"

He has a creepy smile and whatever I was going to say dies on the spot. There's this split second of terrifying forever, then I reach for the keys with every intention of stopping this right now. I have pepper spray on my keychain. This idiot picked the wrong woman to screw with and I want him to know it.

But he covers the keys with his hand before I can get them and calmly asks, "Are you scared?"

"No," I insist. "I just want my damn keys." But my voice is shaky, and my false bravado isn't fooling either one of us.

If anyone else had been in that part of the park on that breezy afternoon, they would have seen an unremarkable old car with two passengers back away from the edge of the ravine and head for the road leading to the park's exit...

I awakened to a huge shot of adrenaline and my heart trying to pound its way out of my chest. Where the hell did that come from? I'm no victim. I've walked away from more than one abusive situation, from more than one person who thought they could treat me like garbage. Physical, mental or verbal, I don't take crap from anyone.

It was still dark out, but at least I felt safe at home. That's what I told myself, anyway. I grabbed my phone off the nightstand and looked at the screen: 4:42 a.m.

Just a nightmare. A very vivid nightmare, one of those really realistic ones, but not real. Yet I was uncharacteristically rattled by it and my heart seemed uninterested in calming down. For a split second I'd been there in my car, wide awake, being driven away by a total stranger and no doubt headed for a very bad ending.

I knew this because I get the "warning to women" emails, the ones that women who work in offices get and forward to their female friends and co-workers. Like the one that tells you not to let a guy force you into your car, to do whatever necessary not to end up in the vehicle with him. Fight, scream, run away, but for God's sake don't get into the car, because if you do the next time you're seen it will be dead in a ditch somewhere. And that's after he made you drive him to an ATM and empty your bank account. Your kidnapper would be the last person to see you alive and the first to see you dead. I remember it also said to run away in a zig-zag pattern if he had a gun, because it makes you a harder target to shoot. That one always stuck in my head, I'm not sure why.

There was a thumping sound and to my disoriented mind it sounded like a car door slamming. Even worse, I was frozen again, just like in the car when I couldn't move, couldn't oh-so-smoothly remove myself from the role of terrified, helpless victim. But it was just the cat jumping onto the bed. Darn you, Cleo.

I lay back onto the pillow while Cleo made herself comfortable on my chest. I scratched behind her ears and was rewarded with the soothing sound of her loud purring. "That was close," I told her. "Too close."

I had to feel like I could have handled the situation better, so I ran through it again in my head.

This part of the park is quiet, shady, and secluded. My ancient Toyota Corolla sits at the edge of a shallow ravine. A silver guardian angel charm and a four-inch long canister of pepper spray dangle from the keychain hanging from the car's ignition.

Both front windows are rolled down, allowing for a pleasant breeze. I sit in the passenger seat because it gives me more room to stretch out. The seat is all the way back and my feet are tucked up on the dash, and I'm busily writing in my journal. Hopes, dreams, to-do lists...important things that I swear I'm going to get to one of these days.

A clean-cut man appears out of nowhere. He calmly opens the driver's side door and slides into my car like he owns it.

"Hey, what are you—"

He has a creepy smile and whatever I was going to say dies on the spot. There's this split second of terrifying forever, then I reach for the keys with every intention of stopping this right now. I have pepper spray on my keychain. This idiot picked the wrong woman to screw with and I want him to know it.

But he covers the keys with his hand before I can get them and calmly asks, "Are you scared?"

"No," I insist. "I just want my damn keys." But my voice is shaky, and my false bravado isn't fooling either one of us.

If anyone else had been in that part of the park on that breezy afternoon, they would have seen an unremarkable old car with two passengers back away from the edge of the ravine and head for the road leading to the park's exit.

As we approach the exit, I remember it's an old car. So old that everything is manual, including the door locks. He can't lock me in. And he has to stop at the gate to make sure he's clear before pulling out of the park, and when he does, I grab my purse and bolt from the car. I run screaming toward a playground about a hundred yards away. Unlike where I had parked, it's heavily populated. After a few strides I remember to zig-zag, even though he doesn't have a gun.

As I flee, I hear him screaming obscenities, cursing me, frustrated at being thwarted.

I still wasn't satisfied. Could it really be that easy? Shouldn't it be more of a challenge?

Another thing, I didn't even know that park. My favorite place to park and hang out is at the top of a hill near the local beach. It's a residential street with a view of the ocean, but one side is empty and fenced off. Years ago, there were houses in the now restricted area, houses that were taken by eminent domain and razed to accommodate an expansion of Los Angeles International Airport. That's the side I parked on. With the houses on the other side of the street, all I'd have to do was make some noise and I'd attract all sorts of attention, even during the day. Ocean-view houses have lots of wives, kids and help at home all day long, no two-income families here. I referred to it as The Perch.

It was a place I could relax, decompress and write in my journal while watching the sun set over the ocean as jets from LAX soared up into the wild blue yonder, heading off to Hawaii, or turning left toward San Diego, or right toward San Francisco. For me, there is nothing more calming than the ocean. I don't know why, but it has never failed to soothe my soul, especially when watching the sun drop lower and lower in the sky until it disappears completely into the horizon. Maybe it's the knowledge that tomorrow the sun will be back up over the ocean again, more dependable than just about anything else in my life, that helps make me feel secure.

My mind drifted back to the park. It just couldn't be that easy. If it were, everyone would get away. Of course, not everyone is as tough as I am. Some people are just born victims. Not me.

Mindlessly petting Cleo, I tried again.

A clean-cut man appears out of nowhere. He calmly opens the driver's side door and slides into my car like he owns it.

"Hey, what are you—"

He has a creepy smile and whatever I was going to say dies on the spot. There's this split second of terrifying forever, then I reach for the keys with every intention of stopping this right now. I have pepper spray on my keychain. This idiot picked the wrong woman to screw with, and I want him to know it.

But he covers the keys with his hand before I can get them and calmly asks, "Are you scared?"

"No," I insist. "I just want my damn keys." But my voice is shaky, and my false bravado isn't fooling either one of us.

He starts the car and grins at me. "Better fasten your seat belt. It's the law."

That's a jolt. He changed his M.O. The seatbelt would make it harder for me to escape. Releasing it would tip him off that I was making a getaway. Only slightly comforted by the sound of a large, purring cat, I forced myself to stay calm and think.

The little car with two passengers heads out of the park and into light traffic. One long block later, it stops at a red light. Nice and law-abiding, nothing to attract attention.

With other cars surrounding us, he can't manhandle me into staying without possibly attracting attention. I quickly grab my purse, undo the seatbelt, and bolt from the car, screaming and dashing around the other stopped cars. Drivers gawk at me as I scramble up the curb and sprint toward the gas station on the corner.

I've forgotten to zig-zag, but as I flee, I can hear him screaming obscenities. Then the signal changes and he peels away, thwarted, and I revel in my victory as a very nice cashier calls 911.

I won, jackass. I could have warned you that you picked the wrong girl to mess with. As for my poor old car, keep it as long as you want. The better to help the cops find you.

Okay, maybe I got a little carried away at the end. Next thing you know, I'd be gearing up for my day in court, prepping my testimony against my imaginary tormentor. *J'accuse,* loser!

But it was enough to calm my nerves and heartbeat, and I dropped back to sleep with a smile as safe, happy purrs sang me a lullaby.

I was dressed to the nines, whatever that means. Even my hair was cooperating. My friend Kaitlin had been gushing about this co-worker she'd been wanting to fix me up with, Jason or Josh or something like that. She'd been working on me for a while and had finally persuaded me to accept an invitation to a work thing. I'd be her plus-one, but if she had her way, I'd be someone else's plus-one by the end of the evening.

It was also early and that wasn't good. Nothing to do but sit and worry if Jason or Josh or whoever would think I was pretty enough, skinny enough, charming enough, sexy enough. Then of course there was the other possibility, that he wouldn't be all that Kaitlin cracked him up to be. And then I started fretting about why I always overthink stuff like this. It was just drinks with a friend and a bunch of her fellow office drones, which they were kind enough to have at Tequila Tony's, my favorite ocean-front bar. And Tony's is pretty laid back, so I was probably overdressed. On the other hand, it was Saturday night, so...and there I go, worrying and expecting the worst, which is stressful and stupid, especially if Kaitlin turned out to be right about Jason or Josh. I figured I'd find out soon enough.

I decided to kill time at The Perch. I would watch the sun go down, feel soothed, and then head to Tony's. I grabbed my journal, purse, and keys, and headed out. When I got to my car, I noticed Cleo watching me from a perch of her own in the front window. I waved to her, getting a silent meow in return.

Parked at The Perch, I tried not to read too much into the fact that I had stayed in the driver's seat, rather than moving to the more spacious passenger side. That way I could prop my journal up against the steering wheel. At least that's what I told myself.

I had the place to myself and tried to bask in the solitude. Usually I preferred it this way. I wasn't the only one who enjoyed The Perch, and the more crowded it got the less relaxing it was. But now it felt eerie.

I glanced at my watch, unable to do anything with the blank journal page in front of me. I had about a half hour of daylight left and needed to kill about the same amount of time so as not to arrive way early and appear too eager (desperate) to Jason or Josh or whatever his name turned out to be. It was also getting stuffy in the car. Reluctantly, I rolled down the windows to get a cross-breeze. It felt good.

I chewed on my pen for a bit, then started scribbling.

Had the creepiest dream—a nightmare, actually. One of those where you wake up and you know it's not real, but it seems so real that you can't just shake it off so easily.

I glanced at the houses across the street, then at the ocean, dotted with sailboats and behind it the sun heading downward. I was surveying my surroundings, annoyed by how nervous I was.

"This is ridiculous." Maybe saying it out loud would break the spell. And it was ridiculous. The entire section to my right is residential, someone would see something, especially with it still being light out. Someone would hear my screams.

And where did *that* come from?

It was nuts—there was not going to be any reason for me to scream at The Perch. It's an upscale neighborhood; I'd been there countless times and had never had a problem, except for that one idiot who'd blasted his music so loud, ruining my peace and quiet that one time. It was a nice neighborhood. I was perfectly safe.

I went back to my journal.

What I need to be focusing on are things that are real and important, like sticking to my diet and updating my resume so I can look for a better job. I'm so bored now, and there's no place for me to move up. I've done this same job for almost four years and I'm ready for a change. I need to stop being so damn lazy and get on this. And tonight I'm meeting Jason/Josh/whatever and I'm going to have fun because, dammit, I deserve it.

He enters the passenger door like he owns the car, so quick and smooth that he's settled in before I can even begin to wrap my head around his presence. We lock eyes. He has a creepy smile and for a second I can't move. But *I'm* in the driver's seat. Me, not him. I reach for the keys, but he gets his hand over them first.

"Are you scared?" he leers

Multiple shots of adrenaline. This is happening. It can't be, but it is. And then I remember, it's an old car. The locks are manual. He can't lock me in.

I scrabble for the door handle, but before I can get it open, he grabs a fistful of my hair and pulls me back toward him. And it isn't his creepy smile I see, but his finger on the trigger of the gun jammed against my forehead.

Oh. He's changed his M.O. again. How did I not consider this scenario? The one where he's armed and I can't move, much less think. What is it I'm supposed to do when he has a gun?

"Start the car," he snarls. "And fasten your seatbelt. Wouldn't want to give anyone a reason to pull us over."

If anyone on the residential side of the street had been watching on that breezy early evening, they would have seen an unremarkable old car with two passengers pull away from the curb and drive slowly away, down the hill toward the sunset.

WHAT'S IN YOUR TANK?

Gerald Martin

Billy Raditz sat at his desk in the Pilough County Sheriff's Office adding up numbers for the annual statistics report. It was not a coveted job. And the desk wasn't even his alone. He shared it in shifts with three other deputies—from a total of seven—who worked for Sheriff Jack "The Rack" Parker. Pilough was a large county in area, but sparse when it came to people.

Billy realized his mind was wandering when two deputies, Smitty and Rob, walked by in front of his desk and interrupted his blank stare at the bulletin board across the room. Smitty darted back into Billy's line of vision and said, "Don't feel bad. Constipated people don't give a crap!"

Billy returned what he hoped passed for a good-natured smile as the two deputies moved away yucking it up. Frankly, Billy was tired of the whole thing. The bulletin board was covered with humorous greeting cards, gross photos, and jokes gleaned from the internet—all having to do with poop in one form or another and aimed at Billy. There was even a "scratch and sniff" card and a really bad attempt at poetry.

Custom had it that the most recently hired deputy got a merciless ribbing after his first screwup or other standout event. Billy's claim to fame had come exactly one week earlier.

Just two short days after he had started working for the department. That was when thirty-two-year-old Caroline Melcher was found strangled to death in the small log home where she lived alone.

Caroline had returned from her off-season break—a common occurrence for workers in a ski town—and had gone directly to a party in a nearby employee housing unit without bothering to unload her car. The local ski crowd deemed the party a great success, but Caroline had left early, alone, to unpack and get ready for work the next day. When she didn't show up the next morning, a friend went to check on her and found her body. The remainder of the day was taken up by a flurry of activity that included EMTs, the entire Sheriff's Department, the State Crime Bureau Forensics Unit, and—though not allowed to cross the yellow crime scene tape—a gaggle of Caroline's ski-bum friends, the editor of the local weekly, and the Catholic priest who admitted he had never met Caroline and didn't even know what her religion might be.

Early on during that fateful day, Sheriff Parker called Billy outside, handed him a shovel, and said, "Follow me." They trudged about twenty feet out from the house to a clearing in the surrounding fir trees.

"See them two round spots with little vegetation?" Sheriff Parker said. "That's where the septic tank is. You know anything about septic tanks, Raditz? Most people make use of them all the time and have no idea how they work. We're interested in that first spot, closest to the house. That's where the sewage comes in. A house this old, it'll be a concrete tank. I'll come back when you have the plug uncovered." And with that, the sheriff left.

Billy didn't have the temerity to ask any questions, seeing as he was one of those who knew nothing about septic tanks. He felt stupid enough without inquiring what kind of plug he was looking for. The other deputies were busy looking for fingerprints, searching the house, scouring the grounds, making casts of tire marks, canvasing the neighborhood, questioning partiers, even doing crowd control. Billy was left with digging a hole, presumably in the pursuit of shit. He wondered if he was being set up for the "last man hired joke," but then dismissed that idea. After all, they were investigating a murder, and Sheriff Parker had looked damned serious. Of course, his demeanor seemed serious about everything.

About a foot down the shovel hit something hard that wouldn't give. It turned out to be the flat top of the septic tank. With the dirt scraped away the plug turned out to be a six-sided chunk of concrete, two feet across, poured in place as part of the top surface of the tank. It had an upside-down "U" bend of rebar stuck in it for a handle.

Billy kept widening the hole until the earth sides couldn't slough down and cover the plug. That's when Sheriff Parker showed up again carrying a long pry bar, a wood meter stick, two cake tins, a big kitchen spoon, and a pair of green rubber gloves. The sheriff set everything down except for the pry bar, which he stuck through the loop of rebar and used it like a lever to break the plug loose. Then he grabbed the rebar and swung the plug off to the side as easily as if it had been a sack of potatoes. That concrete plug was eight inches thick, with the sides sloped inward like you'd carve the top of a Halloween pumpkin.

The first thing Billy noticed as he gazed into the opening where the plug had been was that there wasn't any smell. At least not like he had been expecting. Just a soupy-looking dark liquid about a foot down with greasy scum on top.

Sheriff Parker took a flashlight from his belt and shined it in under the edge of the opening. After a brief look he straightened and handed the light to Billy.

"Raditz, look in there and tell me what you see."

Billy had to bend down close to the opening, but the smell still wasn't that bad. Finally, he said, "Well, sir, it looks like floating turds and toilet paper."

"Most turds sink. But you're right. Back there is a T-shaped baffle over the inlet pipe. I want you to take the meter stick and recover as much of that toilet paper as you can. Do it carefully. Drag it back to the opening and use the spoon to transfer it to those baking tins. Above all, don't try to straighten it out. I want the toilet paper to dry out as near as possible to how it came into the tank."

Now, a week later, Billy was sick and tired of looking at that bulletin board. Some progress had been made on the Caroline Melcher murder case, but he couldn't see how his sojourn into the septic tank had had much to do with it.

Lots of fingerprints had been found in Caroline's home. That was to be expected since she had tons of friends. More importantly, there were no prints on the garrote used to strangle her. It was made from two ski-pole handles, where one end of each wrist loop had been cut free and then sewn back together the same way rock-climbing slings are made. Just the perfect length to loop over someone's head from behind and cross-tighten by a sudden yank on the handles. Premeditation was at play, and likely committed by a local.

Now, the three prime suspects were sitting on a bench just down the hall within Billy's view. They'd been waiting for two hours to be interviewed by Sheriff Parker. Getting restless, they were. No magazines to read; just the glare of washed-out fluorescent light in the windowless hall and opportunities to use the bathroom, which seemed to happen with more frequency as the time passed.

There was Brenda Smith-Thompson, early twenties, trust-funder, and future heiress to the Barrington Tire fortune. Brenda had a habit of dressing down from her background and was known as a troublemaker, usually in the form of instigating bar fights the sheriff's deputies had to break up. She was small though, and Billy couldn't imagine her being able to strangle anybody. She once had an affair with Richard Brent, the second suspect, and there was always the possibility they acted together.

Richard was a realtor, moderately successful, mid-thirties, and plenty big enough to strangle somebody without any help.

The third suspect, Derek Wilcox, was a carpenter, twenty-nine years old, average height, but with a wiry build and a killer tan from working outside and skiing every day in the winter. Derek had a fine-featured face with that odd combination of dark eyebrows under a thatch of blond hair, the latter close-cropped, except on top where it was brushed up into a peak dead-center. Billy thought he looked effeminate, but it was a look the girls went for. Derek was known as quite a ladies' man.

What all three of the suspects had in common was that they had left the party early, alone, after the time Caroline left, and had no alibi for the time frame the medical examiner had set for Caroline's death.

They had one more thing in common. Every time one of them went to the bathroom, they were accompanied by a deputy of the same sex, either Smitty or Rita. Billy found that a strange procedure for suspects who hadn't been arrested yet. Even more so for Smitty to be doing such a menial task, seeing as he was Sheriff Parker's go-to man on big cases. Billy wondered if he would ever be in that position, to have the sheriff's complete confidence. About the only time the sheriff ever cracked a smile was when he was in a confab with Smitty.

Right now, Derek Wilcox was coming out of the bathroom for like the third time, followed as usual by Smitty. Only this time Smitty didn't go back to his desk. Instead, he went directly into the interrogation room adjacent to Sheriff Parker's office, stuck his head back out, and called Richard Brent in.

Brent was in with Sheriff Parker and Smitty for about twenty minutes before leaving with a concerned look on his face.

Next was Brenda Smith-Thompson. Her interview lasted less than ten minutes before she was escorted out by Smitty, who grabbed keys to his patrol car on the way to the front door. Presumably she was getting a ride home and had a smug look on her face.

Sheriff Parker summoned Derek next, and, looking out from the open doorway, said, "Raditz, come in here, too."

When Billy got there, Derek was sitting at the same long table that was used for interrogations, meetings requiring more than three people, the laying out of evidence, consulting with lawyers or the D.A., bamboozling reporters—and more often than not—taking lunch.

Billy stood by the wall off to one side and slightly behind Derek. The sheriff sat down opposite Derek and asked his first question.

"Did you know Caroline Melcher?"

"Sure, I did. Everyone knew Caroline."

"You ever ask her out?"

"Naw. I got all the girls I need without asking her."

"Why? You didn't find her pretty? Intelligent enough?"

"Let's just say she wasn't my type."

"What is your type, Derek?"

"I dunno? All types."

"But not Caroline?" Sheriff Parker let a pause settle in before he added, "Ever get in an argument with her? Have a fight?"

"No." A pause. Then, "That was a long time ago. She was always stirring things up in the bars. Ask anyone."

Sheriff Parker sat there with his hands folded as he watched Derek's eyes slide away. Eventually he said, "Do you know how she was killed?"

"Yes. She was garroted," Derek said. Then he came back stronger, "The word's out all over town. Everyone knows it."

"An unusual choice of words, Derek. Most people when they hear of someone being strangled, they think of bare hands, a rope, maybe a tie. But a garrote?" Parker let out a low chuckle. "Maybe in France. You ever been to France, Derek?"

Derek tried to return the smile. "I dunno. Maybe I seen too

many movies."

"You know, Derek, we never released information about how Caroline was strangled."

There was silence in the room. Billy could smell sweat. Not gym sweat. Fear sweat.

"What kind of movies do you like, Derek? Horror movies?" Parker reached into an evidence box sitting on the table and drew out a plastic bag holding the murder weapon.

Derek barely glanced at it and locked eyes with the sheriff. "I never seen that before! I didn't kill her!"

Just then the door opened, and Rob stood holding it half open. "Derek's lawyer is here," he said.

Cecil Pentworth pushed by the deputy and lumbered into the room, not an inconsiderable task, considering the sheer girth of the man. Cecil was the only trial lawyer in the town, but mostly handled cases of getting people off from DUI charges.

"Jack Parker, my client, is being detained without any justification whatsoever! I insist this charade stop immediately!"

"I wasn't aware Derek had a lawyer," the sheriff said.

"Well, he does now."

"I don't need a lawyer. I haven't done anything!"

"Don't you say another word, son. Not another word. I'm doing this pro bono. Won't cost you a dime."

"Maybe you should listen to him, Derek."

"Well, I suppose it can't hurt. Okay, you're my lawyer, but I tell yah, I'm innocent."

"All right, that's settled," Parker said. "Now sit down, Cecil, and don't get any of that marinara sauce from your tie on my table."

Cecil looked down. There were spots on his tie, but they had dried long ago. He shot daggers at the sheriff and took a seat next to Derek.

"I was just showing your client the murder weapon." Parker spread the plastic bag with the garrote out on the table so the sewn-together webbing strap with a ski pole handle on either end was clearly visible. Cecil's eyes widened a notch.

"Any fingerprints?" he asked.

"Unfortunately, no," Parker said. "And we searched every dumpster in town, and the county dump, and the ski poles belonging to those handles haven't turned up. Yet."

Cecil was on his feet. "Ah ha! Just as I surmised. Not one shred of evidence against my client. Come on, Derek. We are leaving." Cecil put his hand on Derek's shoulder and started for the door.

"Sit your fat ass back down, Cecil!" Parker shouted. "You want, I'll arrest your client right now! Hold him for twenty-four hours. He can keep his trap shut, but I got questions I'm asking one way or another."

"Probable cause, Jack. Probable cause. I may look like a dumb country-hick lawyer to you, but you got any real evidence?"

"Well, here's an interesting tidbit we withheld from the public." Sheriff Parker threw a photograph down on the table. "Whoever murdered Caroline used her lipstick to write 'SLUT' on her bathroom mirror, and we aim to get a handwriting sample from your esteemed client."

"Block lettering," Cecil said. "Block lettering. It won't prove a thing." He didn't look as confident as he made it sound.

"What's more," Parker went on, "a small bit of that lipstick was on the left side of the toilet seat. The seat was down. You'd expect that in a girl's house, but apparently the assailant had taken a dump while he was there." Parker stood and leaned over the table into Derek's face. "I'm surprised you didn't use your own shit to write on her mirror!"

"I didn't do this! Geezus, Cecil, do something."

"He's right, Jack. Either charge my client or let him go."

"Not a bad idea," Sheriff Parker said. He sat back down and pulled out his Miranda card. "Derek Wilcox, you are under arrest for the murder of Caroline Melcher. You have the right to remain silent. You..."

From his position off to the side of the room, Billy watched Derek's expression turn tight-lipped as the rights were being read—and damned if a flicker of a grin didn't sweep over Cecil's face at the same time! That fat old bastard knew if this case went to trial his reputation would spread well beyond the confines of the sleepy seat of Pilough County.

Having read the rights, the sheriff said, "Might as well get this over with, too, while we're at it." He produced a DNA test kit and held it out to Derek. "Inside of your cheek."

Derek took the swab but hesitated. "What about this, Cecil? Do I have to?"

"Afraid so. Everyone arrested in this state has to do it. Even DUI's."

Derek swiped inside of his mouth and put the swab back in the vial. The sheriff set that aside and dug in the evidence box once again. He pulled out seven plastic bags, which he spread out over the table. Billy recognized them right off.

"Know what these are?" Parker said, as his eyes roamed back and forth between Derek and Cecil, watching them lean forward with suspicious and puzzled expressions.

"It's toilet paper," the sheriff went on, "recovered from Caroline's septic tank the morning after she was murdered. Now Caroline had been on vacation for five weeks with no one living in her house, so any toilet paper from before she left would have disintegrated by the time she returned. Therefore, these samples are from anyone who took a dump on the night she was killed. Notice anything interesting about them?"

"This is gross, Jack," Cecil said. "Dried out toilet paper?"

Parker moved the bags into two separate piles. "It's a little-known fact, but sixty-five percent of women are wadders. So, the toilet paper here on the left is Caroline's. But the other two bags are from the murderer. A male. Seventy-three percent of men are folders. No, no, Derek. Don't be afraid. Lean in here and take a good look at them. See how each folded length has several swipes of feces. The heavier swipes were done first, and then the lighter ones. What's more, the swipes are at an angle that says they were done by someone left-handed. Someone like you, Derek, that wipes their ass from the left side."

"Now, hold on, Jack! How would you presume to know that?" Cecil said.

"Because I had Deputy Smith accompany him to the bathroom."

"Oh, so Smitty can see through a stall door now?"

"No, he was watching Derek's feet under the door. You can tell a lot that way. Try it yourself, Cecil, next time you're in a public restroom. Call it research if this case goes to trial."

Cecil tightened his forehead and seemed to mull that over as Parker turned his attention back on Derek.

"The shit on that toilet paper is yours, isn't it, Derek?"

"No, it isn't."

"Derek, it's time to fess up. We will find those ski poles. I have deputies searching your apartment at this very moment. Something will turn up. Gloves. Hair samples. Traces of lipstick. Save us a lot of trouble, Derek. How did it feel when you…"

"Enough!" Cecil banged his hand on the table. He leaned into Derek, practically breathing into his ear. "Don't say a word. All this means is they got nothing. Nothing." He looked at Parker. "My client is innocent."

"Yeah, I didn't do it!"

Parker leaned back and let a moment of silence settle in. Then looked directly at Derek. "We are a small county, Derek, but our agriculture is a big part of the economy. So, I have considerable influence in this state. Let's suppose you go down, Derek, for premeditated murder one." Sheriff Parker held up a finger for Cecil not to interrupt, which he didn't since he was interested himself in hearing where this was going.

"Know where you would wind up? The state prison in Stanton. Stanton is a rough place. There are big-time criminals who know they are being investigated and think the jig is up who will commit a federal crime just so they can serve time in the federal prison in Carterville instead of Stanton. The food is better, TV in the cells, less crowded, better exercise yards, better supervision. Supervision is important, Derek. I hate to think what those cons will do with a pretty boy like you in Stanton."

Derek's hand went up and touched his spiky hairdo. Billy didn't think he was even aware of doing it. His eyes lost whatever arrogance that remained, too.

"People listen to me in this state," Parker went on. "The judges do. The D.A. does. Not always, but a good share of the time. I can see that you do time in the federal prison instead of Stanton. Maybe even get the charge against you reduced to second degree murder. Not easy to do given the kind of garrote used, but impossible without my help. But I need a confession from you, Derek—now. If I have to start jumping through a bunch of hoops to get a case against you, you can forget about any help from me."

"What about that, Cecil?" Derek whined. "Is it true that people commit federal crimes and get caught just so they can keep out of Stanton?"

"I'm not sure," Cecil said. "It's true Stanton is a bad place, but don't you do anything stupid. I need to get bail set and get you out of here before you say another word. So, calm down, son. They don't have any solid proof against you."

"No, but we will have," Parker said, "just as soon as we match his DNA with the DNA on that toilet paper."

Stunned silence. Cecil stared. Derek's hands turned white as he gripped his chair, and color drained from his face.

Then Cecil spoke up. "This is preposterous, Jack. You can't get DNA from a hunk of soggy toilet paper that's been in a septic tank!"

"No?" Sheriff Parker said. "Well, let's just ask Deputy Raditz there. He's fresh out of college. Fresh out of the police academy. He's up on all the latest stuff."

All eyes turned on Billy. He hesitated just a bit before answering, holding his position where he was leaning against the wall, arms folded across his chest. "It's true. You can get reliable DNA from trace amounts of wet feces; but only if it's from someone with blood type O."

Sheriff Parker opened a file folder that was before him on the table and began searching through its contents. Then he stopped and scrutinized one page carefully before looking up. "Well, what do you know? Derek, you are blood type O."

Suddenly Derek was out of his seat. Billy moved forward, ready to take him down and cuff him if need be; but Derek just jittered around behind his chair like a trapped animal. "God damn, Cecil? What am I going to do?"

"Nothing. Do you hear? Nothing!"

"Derek," Sheriff Parker said evenly, "do you have hemorrhoids?"

"What? No."

"Well, you're going to have the worst case ever once you get in Stanton."

Derek squeezed his head, his hands shaking. "All right! All right! I did it!"

"Derek, shut up!"

"No! You shut up, Cecil! I don't want your damn lawyering. I am not going to Stanton! I am not going to Stanton!" Derek collapsed into his chair. "You got to help me, sheriff. I admit it. But she was a slut. Everyone knows it. And the way she treated me..."

"Easy, lad. Just slow down. Tell me what happened."

The following morning Billy was back at his desk working on the same dull statistics, but he was feeling great. He had played an important role in the capture of Caroline Melcher's killer. And the bulletin board was empty. Overnight all the jokes had been taken down.

Sheriff Parker came out of his office, putting his hat on and headed over to Billy's desk. He looked down at what Billy was working on. "Drop that," he said. "Ben Wheeler called in this morning. Said two more cattle disappeared off his ranch last night. I'm going out there myself this time to see what's going on. I want you to ride along with me."

Billy grabbed his hat, feeling elated until he realized the other deputies were solemnly watching him as he followed the sheriff out. That's when he remembered—Parker never reprimanded anyone in front of co-workers.

Outside, Billy got in on the passenger side of the cruiser. The sheriff drove, eyes fixed straight ahead, as stern looking as Billy had ever seen him. He didn't say anything until they were well out of town. When he finally spoke, his voice was flat as a pancake.

"Raditz, where did you come up with that blood type O stuff?"

"Spur of the moment, I guess. I figured if I just answered 'yes' it would have seemed too pat. Like I was just parroting what you wanted me to say."

"Did you even stop to consider how that might screw things up?"

"Well, the majority of people are blood type O, and most don't even know their blood type." Oh, man, that sounded lame. Billy quickly added, "I'm sorry, Sir. I won't let it happen again."

"No. It was good," the sheriff said. "It lent a certain verisimilitude to the proceedings."

That last sentence was delivered with the best W.C. Fields imitation Billy had ever heard. He couldn't help but laugh. Maybe from relief. Certainly so, when he saw the sheriff was smiling, too.

So, when Billy got his mirth under control, he got up the courage to ask a question he had been wondering about all morning. "Sir, do you think he'll get away with it?"

"Well, even a lawyer like Cecil could get that confession thrown out; and there will be better sharks than him circling the waters. But no, I think we will find more evidence. Plus, in a small state like this, once word gets out, it's hard to find a jury that can disregard everything they are instructed to. Raditz, do you know how I got my nickname?"

"Yes, sir. They say when you interrogate someone it's like putting them on the rack."

"An exaggeration, that." After a pause, the sheriff added, "I suppose you've figured out I don't have a clue what Derek's blood type is?"

"Yes, sir."

"So, Raditz, how are you finding police work?"

"It's great. I've learned more in one week than all the time in college."

"Yeah? Give me an example."

"Well, like you can get DNA from wet toilet paper that's been in a septic tank. I find that really amazing."

"Billy, if we're going to keep working cases together, you have got to stop believing in crap like that."

BAHNHOF FRIEDRICHSTRASSE

Cornelia Feye

Vega's dream of seeing the ancient Babylonian Ishtar Gate was about to come true. She would see the cobalt blue tiles of the forty-six-foot-high monument with her own eyes. She could finally experience, not just imagine, how it felt to walk through the ceremonial gate that had been dedicated to the goddess Ishtar five hundred years before the birth of Christ.

In 1983 the Ishtar Gate stood inside the Pergamon Museum in East Berlin and unfortunately the Berlin Wall stood solidly between East and West. Vega had seen the Wall's west side, covered with graffiti proclaiming the world is too small for walls or "*Auf die Dauer Fällt die Mauer*" and other slogans. Spray-painted images of Trabis, tiny East German cars, broke through the barrier into freedom. But the east side of the Wall consisted of a sandy, empty death strip, closely spaced watch-towers manned by snipers, two barbed-wire fences, and a patrol road running along the twelve-foot-high concrete barrier.

East Berliners lived as prisoners in a gray city behind an Iron Curtain, while West Berliners enjoyed their colorful and culturally diverse island embedded in the giant block of East

Germany. In the division of the city after World War II, the museum island, including the Pergamon Museum, had landed on the east side of the Wall. Vega, who lived in West Germany, had to travel through East Germany to West Berlin first. She could reach West Berlin from Southern Germany only by plane or by driving on one of the Transit Roads—roads that led from West Germany to West Berlin through East Germany without being part of it. She opted for the transit roads, because they were the cheapest solution.

After driving through East Germany nonstop for hours, she reached the transit station Dreilinden, the entry point into West Berlin. East German border patrol agents conducted a slow and thorough process of controlling her visa and timing, making sure she had not stopped along the way. Military tanks, rocket launchers and an oversized bronze sculpture of the Socialist leader Walter Ulbricht in the middle divider between lanes provided a diversion during the wait, as well as propaganda for East Germany's military might.

The next day Vega embarked on her trip to the other side of the Wall to the Pergamon Museum. As a Wessie, Vega could visit East Berlin, but East Berliners didn't have the freedom to visit the West. Despite her advantage, crossing to the other side was not an easy operation. At the subway station Bahnhof Friedrichstrasse, once again she had to endure a lengthy checkpoint, get another visa, another time stamp, and exchange West German Marks for East German currency. After enduring this ordeal, she finally stepped onto *Unter den Linden,* the glamorous Main Street of Berlin.

Vega approached the Pergamon Museum excited and disappointed at the same time. The admission of one Eastmark and seventy-one Pfennige for two of the greatest architectural monuments of antiquity seemed like a bargain. But the museum looked dingy and the climate control did not work. However,

Ishtar's ceremonial gate proved to be as glorious as she had hoped and dreamed. She walked along the cobalt blue-glazed walls, with ceramic relief sculptures of Aurochs, sacred bulls, snake-headed dragons dedicated to the god Marduk, and Ishtar's golden lions at eye level. Despite the bleak surroundings, she felt transported back in time and space to ancient Babylonia. Once these gilded animals had guarded and glorified King Nebuchadnezzar and the goddess Ishtar.

Underneath the gate, Vega had to crane her neck to look up at the towering arch. The enormous structure had been excavated and disassembled in Babylon and rebuilt with its original indigo-tiled bricks inside the Pergamon Museum in the 1930s, before the division of Berlin. Transcending time and space, it formed a portal to a different world.

Leaving the museum, she wondered what to do with the rest of the twenty-one Eastmarks and twenty-nine Pfennige she had been forced to exchange. They were worthless in the West. A cup of coffee and a huge piece of cream pie on Alexanderplatz only used up two Eastmarks and thirteen Pfennige, and the elderly waitress rejected the generous tip Vega tried to give her. "Tips are undesirable here," the waitress stated surprisingly.

Wandering around Alexanderplatz, Vega considered taking the elevator up the tall TV tower with its giant sphere balanced high up in the air, but the lines were too long, and she wanted to be back in West Berlin in time for dinner with friends. She entered a music store for classical records and music cassettes. No rock or pop music there. Young East Berliners coveted recordings by punk bands like the *Dead Kennedys* or *Fine Young Cannibals*, because they were hard to get. Instead she purchased three classical cassettes—a recording of the Goldberg Variations by Bach, the Brandenburg Concertos, and excerpts from Wagner's *Ring der Nibelungen* recorded by the Berlin Philharmonic. Relieved of some East German currency, she returned to Bahnhof Friedrichstrasse to cross back to the West.

During the tedious crossing Vega wondered whether the

drabness of East German aesthetics was deliberate or by default. The uniforms, the shabby furniture, the color of the walls, the squeaking turnstiles, and the smell in the station dulled her senses, and induced a strong desire to be somewhere else—anywhere but here.

When she reached the turnstile a bespectacled border guard demanded her passport and visa. He conducted the normal procedure of checking her pockets and purse. The guard glared at Vega over his old-fashioned glasses and ordered in a broad accent, "Move over this way." He still held her passport and purse.

"Why? What's the matter?" Vega asked with alarm. An icy stare was her answer.

"Step to the side," the guard repeated, and two bulky female guards approached. Flanking her on both sides, they escorted her through a door, down two flights of stairs, and finally into a small cell.

"Where are you taking me? What have I done?" Vega protested. In stony silence, her guards pushed her into the cell. The door fell into its lock behind her with an echoing sound, and Vega was alone.

Her first impulse was to bang on the door and scream to be let out, asking why she was detained. But it wouldn't have any effect. She wanted to tell them she was a West German citizen, they couldn't do this to her, her government would find her and get her out. But that was probably not going to happen. Nobody would look for her for a while or risk a diplomatic incident because of an insignificant tourist. Her heart started racing and panic threatened to choke her. With shaking hands, she steadied herself against the wall, while all blood drained from her brain.

She sat down on a wooden bench and looked around. Green washable paint covered the walls up to eye level. She saw air ducts high on the wall, but no windows so far underground. A naked light bulb dangled from the ceiling in the middle of the room. A wooden table with a chair and a typewriter stood in one corner. That was it.

Vega looked at the green walls and remembered reading that it was easier to wash blood off green paint than cement. She shuddered. There was something she should be doing. But what?

Assessing her situation was a start. She was locked in a cell, three stories underneath Bahnhof Friedrichstrasse. She did not know why. She had no idea how long they would hold her. She didn't know of any way she could make contact with the outside world, and she had to go to the bathroom. The cup of coffee from Alexanderplatz sat on her bladder. This was the most claustrophobic space she had ever been in. Her possessions, including her passport, had been confiscated. She could simply fall into the cracks between Eastern and Western bureaucracy and rot in this cell.

Instant panic rose again. How had she landed from the awe-inspiring lofty Ishtar Gate, one of the Seven Wonders of the World, into a cramped prison cell with peeling paint? Her heart raced and her head pounded, but she realized at this moment there was nothing she could do.

Vega began to calm down a bit by analyzing her immediate surroundings. Her bottom, back, and shoulders were sore from sitting on the hard, wooden bench. She moved it in front of the green wall and leaned against it. Better. Air came in through the air vents along the ceiling; not very fresh, but breathable, and the temperature was pleasant. Not too hot and not too cold. Even locked up, she still had space to move. At least she was not confined in a cramped cage. She also had light, albeit just a naked bulb hanging from the ceiling. Funny, Vega thought, how I suddenly appreciate the basic necessities I normally take for granted.

She didn't know how long she would have to stay in this

cell. Possibly her worst nightmare would come true and they would forget about her down here. Nobody from her family would find her, and the East and West German bureaucracies often failed to communicate. She would become a non-entity lost in the shuffle. Panic spread throughout Vega's body. Her heart raced and blood roared in her ears.

It was possible they wouldn't find her, but unlikely. At this moment it didn't matter, whether she panicked or not. For the first time in her life she had no options. Vega took a deep breath and let this thought sink in. Surprisingly it opened up a space she never knew existed. There was nothing else to do but succumb to the moment. Just be in this moment without thinking ahead to the next one.

She remembered the blue-glazed Ishtar Gate. The glow of the deep cobalt tiles combined with the height of the gate became a portal in her mind. It transported her to a place where time stretched, and her cell seemed more spacious.

She saw herself as a small speck in the bowels of Berlin's Bahnhof Friedrichstrasse. Subway trains and tracks criss-crossed above, and she heard their faint rumble in the night. In her mind's eye, she saw people in the train wagons moving across the city. People got out at stations, moved through turnstiles, walked down dark streets under streetlights and blinking neon signs. It had turned dark since her arrest—how long ago? Vega checked her watch. Only one hour had passed. Better not check the time, or else she would get trapped in the panic again, worrying about how long she'd have to stay. Better to focus back on the tracks.

She zoomed down to the station, and mentally traveled down the corridors until she arrived back at her cell, exactly where she had started.

As if on cue, a key turned in the lock and a sturdy green-uniformed East German policewoman strode in. She threaded a form into the typewriter on the table in the corner and sat down on the wooden chair with her back to Vega.

"Why am I here? When can I get out? My family will be worried. I need to send a message."

The woman did not answer. Didn't even look around.

"Name? Date of birth? Address?" she asked curtly.

"You have my passport. It's all in there," Vega answered.

"Name? Date of birth? Address?" the woman repeated, a little louder this time.

Vega answered; asked again, "Why am I here?" Again, no response.

"What were you doing in East Berlin? Recount each of your actions and purchases," the policewoman demanded.

Vega began with the museum, the cup of coffee at Alexanderplatz, the purchase of the music cassettes. She failed to mention a conversation she had had with a young East German family in the café. A mother with her little baby in an old-fashioned stroller implored Vega to give her some West German Marks so she could buy baby powder, unavailable with Eastern currency. Vega had relented and given her a few marks. The Stasi could not know about that, could they? Of course, it was strictly forbidden to interact with East Berliners.

The policewoman finished typing, pulled the form from the typewriter, and got up to leave.

"Wait, I need to get out of here. I have to go to the bathroom," Vega pleaded.

The woman ignored her, opened the door and left. Vega heard the keys turn in the lock. She sank back onto her bench. This was bad, very bad. What had she done to land her in a prison cell? Was it a crime to like classical art and music? Panic started to rise again. Vega felt her heartbeat accelerating in her constricted chest. She observed her own fear and how her thoughts became muddled and her breath came out short and shallow. Observing her physical reactions without judgment, they subsided slowly.

When Vega returned to the present moment, she began to move with time—inside time—and therefore didn't feel its passage. Only two hours ago she had walked through an ancient gate as Babylonians had done twenty-five hundred years before. Time had become meaningless. She had entered its stream. It felt like entering a river in an inner tube. Floating along, she relaxed. Her surroundings didn't matter anymore, because she occupied an inner space. She stopped wondering what to do next or what would happen to her. She had arrived. For the first time in her life, she was really truly present.

Grateful for the hard, wooden bench, Vega felt it grounded her and confirmed the reality of her situation. I have arrived, she thought.

As Vega sat suspended in her moment, the door opened and the policewoman returned. She looked at Vega with mild surprise.

"You can go," she announced.

"What?" Vega scrambled to her feet.

"Here is your passport and purse."

"Thank you." Vega took her belongings.

"We had to confiscate your cassettes."

"Oh?"

"They could have contained espionage information," the woman declared without any expression or intonation. "It is a crime to take cassettes in or out of East Berlin," she added for emphasis.

"I did not know."

The woman looked straight ahead, standing in the open door. Vega could have hugged her. With as much dignity as she could manage, she took hold of her belongings and walked out. She ascended floor after floor, stairs after stairs, and emerged into a mild night on the Western side of Bahnhof Friedrichstrasse. She looked at her watch.

The timeless moment was over. She was back on a schedule. She had spent three hours in the cell. Three hours, three cassettes. While she had sat on her wooden bench, listening to the ventilation system, the Stasi officers had obviously listened to her Bach Goldberg Variations, and Brandenburg concertos, expecting to hear confidential espionage information. Vega smiled. She hoped they had enjoyed the music.

SANDMAN

B.J. Graf

Malibu, 2041

At five-forty-five on a cool cloudy morning surveillance-drone Daedalus spotted something strange. A man lay stretched out near the briny line of sea foam, one hundred feet from the Broad Beach security office. With the tide devouring the thin line of walkable public sand at the water's edge, no beachgoers set foot on Broad Beach this early. Security guard George Nizam shut down the drone. As he went to investigate, the sky overhead faded in from black to cobalt, painting the hills a crimson pink, then dissolving to a pale grey.

"Hey," George shouted, his hands cupped like a megaphone. His feet made gritty crunching sounds as he walked in the pebble-strewn ground. "You're on private land. You can't sleep here." His shoes sank into wet sand, tattooing canvas and leather with brine.

The guy didn't stir. George pushed his glasses up onto his thatch of dark brown hair and narrowed his eyes for a better look.

The sleeping man lay covered in sand up to his neck, a battered felt hat angled over his face. George bent down and lifted the hat. And gasped.

He was staring at the instantly recognizable face of Josh Barton, owner of the white contemporary two houses down, and the biggest star in Hollywood.

George made two calls on his glove phone. The second was to 911. The first—to L.A.'s top e-rag, U-Star, which would pay well for the scoop.

"Josh Barton dead." Homicide Special Detective Eddie Piedmont glanced at his partner as he turned the nose of the black sedan into the Broad Beach security office parking lot. "I can't remember when he wasn't a huge star."

"And only forty." Eddie's partner, Shin Miyaguchi, had turned forty-four last September. "You remember that time in *Iced* when his partner got killed, and he went to see the widow? Man, that broke me up." Shin ran his hand over his shaved head.

With a slow half-nod Eddie eased the sedan into a cramped parking space.

The detectives sat in silence as the engine shut off. Shin resolved to eat better and exercise more. Twenty-nine-year old Eddie was remembering the day he'd bought the ten-year-old, pre-owned version of the Porsche Josh Barton had raced up the coast in the detective thriller *Silver or Lead.* Eddie'd eaten peanut butter sandwiches for breakfast and lunch two years in a row so he could afford that car. The way the car made Eddie feel made the sacrifice worthwhile.

"Barton," Eddie said, "was cool." But what Eddie meant was *he made us look cool.* Only now Josh Barton was dead.

As he stepped onto the tarmac an ocean breeze ruffled his thick, immaculately cut, black hair. Without breaking stride, Eddie buttoned the jacket of his fine, charcoal-grey, Italian suit.

Behind them, the sedan's pulsing arterial-red and neon-blue lights shut off in a heartbeat. Police sponsor Firestone's LED logo, running 'round the base of the sedan doors, dimmed.

"The guy was an industry." Shin squeezed into his tan off-the-rack suit jacket. "You know Barton's listed on the Nasdaq?"

Eddie nodded. His contacts darkened, turning his ice-blue eyes black in the sun. "His IPO shot through the roof last month."

Investors who bought into the biggest stars could make or lose good money, according to the points on a star's latest contract or advertising deals. Naturally, the stars made more, one of the privileges inherent in the celebrity pantheon.

"S&P Capital still lists Barton as the number-one lead." The stats floated in the L-shaped space between thumb and forefinger on Shin's glove phone. "Bet his shares tumble any second." Shin and Eddie walked toward the set of wooden stairs leading down to the beach.

"They'll rebound," Eddie said. "Fame's fickle, but 'cool' never goes out of style."

James Dean was proof of that. That icon still sold years after his death while other stars were forgotten before their bodies cooled. Death wasn't as democratic as the poets claimed.

Uniformed officers, green lights of their helmet-cams on, stood sentinel on the perimeter. One signed the detectives into his glove-phone log.

Both detectives strode through the virtual crime-tape, a yellow LED beam streaming *Do Not Cross* in four languages. The virtual tape rippled and reassembled itself once Eddie and Shin passed.

Forensics officers combed the terrain. Eddie took in the area from the line of luxury smart homes clustered on the hillside behind him to the corpse ahead. He recognized the ME/coroner, a forty-something woman with caramel skin and flame-colored hair, kneeling by the body.

"Heart failure," Coroner Soledad Garcia said in answer to Shin's query as to the preliminary cause of death. Dr. Garcia tucked a loose strand of hair back into the neat bun at the nape of her neck as she glanced up. "Around midnight. Most likely drug-induced. Barton's insta-tox scan read positive for massive amounts of Green Ice and Blue Lotus." Garcia showed the detectives Barton's level of extreme intoxication.

Green Ice was the street name for a synthetic heroin more potent than fentanyl. Blue Lotus was a dangerous new variety of genetically engineered spice. The lethal cocktail had sent many a body to the morgue prematurely.

By eight a.m. the thick marine layer still blanketed the area. But forensics had dug the actor's body out in preparation for transport to the morgue.

Barton's famous face had turned yellowish like a badly painted display in the Hollywood Wax Museum. A thin veil of sand still dusted his naked chest and blue board shorts, but there was no bruising or any other sign of foul play. Only a slight skin abrasion on the left forearm, which the coroner put down to the sand.

"What about the drugs?" Eddie asked the coroner. "Shot or skinned?"

"Skinned." Fingers gloved in blue latex, Garcia parted the dead star's strands of wavy blond hair and pointed to a small dermal patch behind his right ear.

"Point-fifteen's a lot of Ice and Spice for one dermal," Eddie said.

"Not if he was high already," Shin said. "Users OD all the time."

"Yeah," Eddie said, his tone skeptical. "But they don't bury themselves in sand. Barton had help."

"The e-rags got wind of Barton's death," Shin said. "Shares of his stock are tumbling."

Eddie nodded. Despite additional blue-suiters stationed around the site to keep paparazzi at bay, a horde of tabloid cameras pressed up against the cordon, recording footage for download to rabid fans.

"More than rumors flying, too." Eddie pointed at a few of the drones that larger e-rag operations, like U-Star and TMZ, had launched from outside the perimeter. Security drones launched inside ran the e-rag models out. One drone that refused to be corralled was blasted from the sky before it got above the scene. The air smelled of singed metal and burning plastic. The hiss and crackle reminded Eddie of electronic bug-zappers.

"This is why I hate celebrity cases," Shin said.

A half-smile flitted across Eddie's face. "Let's just find out who buried Barton ahead of schedule. Somebody must have seen something. Who found the body?"

The green light on her helmet-cam bobbing, a blue-suiter gestured to pudgy George Nizam.

George walked the detectives through it.

"Security footage? These houses must have cameras." Shin indicated the luxury smart homes planted along the beach.

"There're twenty between Barton's house and the security office." George indicated the location of each. "There was a private party on the beach last night. About fifty people were milling around, counting Mr. Barton."

"Twelve of the cameras show Barton and a woman walking from the beach to his house around seven," said the uniformed officer. "There's nothing showing Barton returning to the beach between seven and nine."

"And after nine?" Shin asked. "The coroner said TOD was around midnight."

"There's nothing after nine," George said. "Not until five-thirty a.m. when the cameras came back on."

"What happened to the cameras between nine and five-thirty?" Eddie said.

"The owners don't like us to advertise it," George said, pursing his lips, "but sometimes they shut down the system—like when there's a party. There's a privacy bypass code. All of them have access."

Eddie shot Shin a look. "Who shut it down last night?"

"Mr. Ellison." George pointed to the grey Cape Cod south

of Barton's home.

Tech billionaire Ellison was the host of the previous night's bacchanal. Questioning revealed Ellison had frolicked in the waves with a curvy brunette once his wife had taken her Ambien and retired for the night. The host claimed he'd been so swept up by the brunette's charms he didn't even remember seeing Barton. Ellison only remembered to turn the cameras back on when his smart house sounded his wife's wake-up alarm. He had, however, remembered to take some naked holo selfies with the lady. The time code and the brunette both backed up Ellison's account, which meant the detectives still had a big fat hole in the timeline and no idea who'd turned Josh Barton into the Sandman.

"Who's the woman with Barton on the tape?" Eddie asked. The woman in the footage was tan and toned. "Do we need facial recognition software?"

"No," the security guard replied. "That's Petra, Barton's wife."

"Trophy wife." Shin looked up from his glove-phone, where he was sifting through WebBoards. "Barton's third. He's a man of set habits: trades in his car every year and his spouse every six."

"Smells like a prenup," Eddie said. "Big payoffs kick in at year seven. We should find out how long Barton and his trophy have been married. Let's check out spouses one and two while we're at it. See if either of them was at the party. Maybe somebody wasn't too happy about being dumped for a newer model."

"We'll need a guest list, too," Shin told the security guard. "But first we have to give Mrs. Barton the bad news. God, I hate this part of the job."

Eddie was already ten feet ahead, walking toward the white contemporary house five hundred meters west along the beach. Shin sped up.

By now paparazzi swarmed the site's perimeters. Wailing

fans had joined the throng, jostling for a view of the proceedings. Some brought flowers, others had candles and pictures of the star smothered with lipstick kisses. Eddie cut through the wailing mass with a curt "no comment."

As they passed through the gauntlet of security cameras surrounding Josh Barton's house, Eddie and Shin had their badges out, their faces turned up toward the entryway camera perched high above the door. They rang the bell. After a few moments the door opened, revealing the woman from the tape whom the security guard had identified as Petra, the dead star's wife. Her straight black hair, which fell to her clavicle, looked uncombed, and her high-cheekboned face was makeup-free. She wore a hastily tied sarong that fell just above the knee.

"Ms. Barton?" Shin asked.

"Mrs.," the young woman corrected. The anxious look she gave the detectives and the constant pinging of her glove phone told Eddie and Shin they weren't the first to deliver bad news.

"It's about your husband," Shin said.

"He's not here." With a glimpse of detective-gold, fear had crept into Petra's voice. "He had a six-a.m. call time."

Eddie was just about to ask her the last time she'd seen her husband when a brand-new Mercedes 3000-XL roared into the drive. The door blew open and out sprang Josh Barton.

Eddie blinked at the famous face of the movie star. Shin's mouth gaped open like a dying codfish before he remembered to snap it shut.

The green-eyed movie star wore faded jeans and a long-sleeved white oxford shirt, untucked. His face was still in makeup. Barton froze, taking in the detectives on his doorstep. He slammed the car door then strode up the drive, the heels of his custom-made cowboy boots clicking on tarmac.

Even in high-heeled cowboy boots, screen god Barton's head just reached Eddie's chin.

"What's going on?" Josh said. "It's a zoo out there. Twitter's blown up, and it's all over the news I died from an overdose. I don't even use."

Eddie pulled up a holo photo of the Sandman on his glove phone and showed it to the star. "This man was found dead on the beach near your house this morning."

Josh glanced at the photo. His smile evaporated and he went pale under his tan. There was a sharp intake of breath before he spoke.

"Trey," Josh Barton said, angling his body so his wife could view the floating image too. "Oh, God, no wonder. It's Trey."

And then Eddie knew. "You have a MIM?" he said.

Josh Barton nodded.

MIMs was the brand name for the elite celebrity doubles hired to attend some of the surplus events that top-tier celebrities couldn't. It was a cutting-edge PR program the police had been briefed on only a month ago. Regulation hadn't yet made its way through the bureaucracy. MIMs were nano-surgically altered to be mirror images of the stars they doubled, but Eddie had never knowingly seen one in the flesh before now. Eyes ricocheting between the dead MIM's picture and the actor, Eddie was impressed by how closely they resembled each other.

"Oh, my god," Petra Barton echoed, peering at the image. The shouted questions of the paparazzi made her glance up. "Come in," Petra said, wheeling around and ushering the detectives inside, away from the noise and prying lenses. She closed the door behind them all.

Eddie followed the couple into the house. "What's Trey's last name?"

"Lyptos." Josh Barton collapsed onto a soft leather sofa of pale gray. He gestured for the detectives to take seats in the squat armchairs opposite. "Trey Lyptos." He sat on the edge of the sofa, head cradled in his hands, elbows on knees. "I can't believe he's dead. It's horrible."

"Josh," Petra interrupted in a soft tone of concern. "Is there someone we should call? Maybe we should take care of the funeral arrangements."

"What?" Josh said after a moment's pause. "Oh, yeah, Rick, call Rick. My manager," he explained to the detectives as Petra padded to the kitchen barefoot, her head shaking in disbelief. "What happened?" he asked Eddie. "Was it drugs like the reports said?"

Eddie and Shin shared a glance. "We won't know till the autopsy," Eddie said.

"Rick's line is busy," Petra called out from the kitchen. "I'll keep trying. And we've got to call your PR agent. They'll have to issue a statement. Oh, my god. Everybody still thinks it's you who died. On top of everything, your stock cratered."

"It'll rebound once word gets out that I'm fine," Josh said, making a dismissive gesture with his hand. "But Trey..."

Eddie guessed that the public relations agent would issue some bullshit statement about mistaken identity on the part of the police. He knew from last month's departmental briefing that publicity firms were not eager to inform the public about MIMs. They preferred to sustain the illusion that A-list stars could appear at events everywhere simultaneously, like Santa Claus.

"Why was Mr. Lyptos on your private beach yesterday?" Eddie asked. "Was he working?"

Josh took his hands off his head and looked at Eddie. "Yeah," he said. "The Ellisons next door had a party they wanted me to attend."

A few moments later Petra returned from the kitchen with a glass of iced tea and three cups of coffee on a tray. She set the tray down on the driftwood coffee table and sat next to her husband.

"Thanks, babe." Josh tapped his chest as he looked at his wife. A light double-tap over his heart.

"Who hired Mr. Lyptos to double for you last night?" Eddie asked. "You, the host, or your PR firm?"

"I did," Josh said. "Last week I agreed to go to the thing,

but I didn't feel up to it yesterday. Trey went instead."

"You mentioned drugs earlier," Eddie said. "Was Mr. Lyptos known to have a drug problem?"

"That was in the past." Josh ran his hands through his already-tousled hair, making the pale blond strands stand up like white caps on a windy sea. "I never would have asked him if I'd thought anything like this would happen. I thought Trey was clean."

Petra laid her right hand on Josh's left in a gesture of reassurance. "I bet the Ellisons offered him some primo shit he couldn't pass up."

"Yeah," Josh said. "Too much temptation. I should've known."

Eddie let the couple fill the air with their informative domestic speculation. He and Shin both made mental notes to check out the Ellisons for drug-related histories.

"You always felt sorry for Trey," Petra said to Josh.

Eddie looked up. "Why's that?"

Josh took a long pull on his iced tea then set the glass quietly back down on the coffee table. "Do you remember that web series *Borders*? From 2035?

Eddie shook his head.

"I do," Shin said. "That was the one with the big family. The Fronteras. One brother was a cop in San Diego. One was a banger in with the cartels." Shin's bass voice went even deeper as he mimicked the show's sing-song promo. "There are red lines in every life. Borders where you have to choose. Cross or don't."

Josh nodded. "Trey played the transgender kid brother. He *made* that series. Trey should have been a star."

"What happened?" Eddie said.

"The series got canceled, and the fans forgot." Josh played with the melting cubes of ice in his tea, digging out the slivers of mint and mango inside. "I think that's why he became a MIM." He met Eddie's eyes. "I just wanted to help the guy out. He was so damn talented."

"You see why I love this man?" Petra's eyes misted over as she listened to Josh eulogize the dead MIM.

Glancing from Josh to Petra, Eddie thought wife number three might have more staying power than the first two.

"I'm lucky," Josh said, flashing that charismatic smile that lit up screens across the world. Then just as quickly as it had appeared, the smile faded, replaced by a soft faraway look. "Trey wasn't. He just missed it all. The fans, the fame, especially the fame. Fame's addictive."

"Did Mr. Lyptos have any enemies?" Shin asked.

Josh looked up, startled. "Wasn't Trey's death accidental?"

"That much Ice 'n Spice," Shin said, "we have to cover the bases. Did he?"

The movie star shook his head.

"One more thing," Eddie said, his voice even. "Is there anyone who might have wanted *you* dead, Mr. Barton?"

Josh looked from one detective to the other. "You think somebody was trying to kill *me*?"

Petra looked up from her glove phone. "And they murdered Trey by mistake?" The blood drained from her face.

Eddie cocked his head. "Did the host, Mr. Ellison, or anyone besides you and your wife, know your MIM went to the party instead of you?"

Josh shook his head. "It was last minute, like I said."

All four sat there in silence as the unspoken sank in.

"It wouldn't be a bad idea to hire extra security for a while," Eddie said. "As a precaution."

"We should go," Shin said a few moments later. "We'll be in touch." The two detectives got contact info and headed back to the beach.

"MIMs," Eddie said when he and Shin were twenty-five feet away from Barton's door. "Just when I think the world can't get any crazier another rabbit hole opens up under our feet."

"Only on the surface," Shin said. Both men had seen a lot in their time, most of it dark and not particularly deep. Money and sex topped the list of motives for murder.

"Wouldn't hurt to see if anybody at the party cashed in Barton's stock and made a killing," Eddie said as the two detectives got into their car and headed downtown.

They were looking at a long slog. There were more than fifty people to interview, including Barton's ex-wives. Eddie had just finished his call to the morgue to update the coroner about the MIM when Shin's phone pinged again.

"Oh, my god," he said, "Pull up U-Star. It's Barton's ex."

The star's first ex-wife, former B-list actress Cary Giudice, was all over the net. Eddie found himself staring at the ravaged face of an Ice addict in the middle of her drug-fueled rant. Time code indicated she'd started to live stream it only moments before.

"I supported you for years before you made it big, Josh! I gave up everything for you." She made staccato jabbing motions. "That Toyota spot you didn't think was right for *your* image? And the role in that *Fast and Furious* spin-off? I could've been a star. Fuck it, I even aborted our child because you weren't ready to be a father!" She leaned into the camera. Her voice got loud and shrill enough to make the air bleed. "The world should know America's Hero is a prick. I have nothing left, Josh. You took my life! Now you got yours."

There wasn't even time to send a squad car before Cary Giudice stuck the barrel of a nine-millimeter in her mouth and blew her brains out for all the digital world to see.

"Jesus," Shin said. "You think she killed Barton?"

"Means and opportunity," Eddie said. "It tracks. What a mess." Cary Giudice hadn't even known it was the MIM, not her ex-husband, who died.

The ex-wife's crazy taped confession-suicide went viral in seconds. Social media that carried the live stream dropped two and a half percent on Nasdaq within minutes. There was a frenzied sell-off of Barton's cratered stock.

Eddie looked at his partner. *Another rabbit hole.* The two detectives continued their drive without a word.

At the morgue Coroner Soledad Garcia confirmed that the deceased had indeed died from a massive drug overdose. The pro-forma scan of his identity chip, embedded in the dead man's forearm and standard issue since Homeland Security had begun requiring them in 2035, was a match for Trey Lyptos.

With Cary Giudice's taped confession, it was looking like the case would be closed by the day's end.

By the time the detectives made it back to Homicide Special, Barton's publicity team had issued a statement. Eddie'd been right. They didn't mention anything about MIMs. Just that the deceased Trey Lyptos looked a lot like Josh Barton. The story was that in her drug-fueled mania, Cary Giudice had confused the two and murdered an innocent man before taking her own life. The police were blamed for the initial panic over the star's death, even though it had been the security guard who leaked the story.

Seated at his desk in Homicide Special, Eddie replayed Cary Giudice's rant against Josh Barton.

"I ran down both Bartons and the dead ex-wife's social media pages," Shin said. "Take a look."

The litany of complaints against Josh Barton was long and colorful.

"Barton was a selfish asshole," one anonymous former assistant posted online. "I worked eighteen-hour days for him. He promised me an associate producer credit and a huge bonus. Then he fired me—right before the holidays!"

"I know you're not supposed to, like, shit on the dead," posted Gripsunited23. "But Barton kept the whole cast and crew of *Iced* waiting for like three hours while he sat in his trailer and watched a Rams's game. Fucking disrespectful."

The detectives knew stars weren't what they seemed. Nobody was. But Giudice and the other complainers circling Josh

Barton always seemed to have an axe to grind—jealous lovers or assistants who'd violated confidentiality contracts in exchange for a payoff or book deal. Against that Eddie and Shin balanced the counterweight of other stories circling the star-glowing accounts of compassion, some even of genuine heroism.

"Josh Barton gave me a two-hundred-dollar tip on a ten-dollar check," one elderly waitress streamed.

"He got my son into rehab," Desperatefather52 posted. "And paid for it himself."

"People either loved or hated him," Shin said.

"Yeah." Eddie nodded. "How did Barton strike you?"

"He seemed okay. A lot of stars are too self-absorbed to notice the problems of 'the help'."

Eddie nodded again. Josh Barton had shown compassion and empathy for the dead MIM.

As they slogged through the kind of police work that never made it into a Josh Barton movie, Eddie let a clip of *Silver or Lead* play in the background. Eddie knew the movie was bullshit, but he also knew the lines by heart. Only now the movie failed to work its magic. On impulse Eddie pulled up an episode of *Borders*, the Lyptos series. Eddie felt like it was the least he could do for the poor MIM who hadn't even died his own death.

It took a second to recognize Trey Lyptos. He was just a kid, and this was years before he'd surgically morphed into Josh Barton. Ironically, Trey was a better actor than Josh Barton. He made you believe he *was* this kid brother he was playing. Eddie had always thought great actors, like criminals, were great liars, but it hit him now that actors told the truth. The truth wrapped inside a fake setup. The show was awful, but Trey Lyptos wasn't.

He just wasn't a star. And Eddie saw why Trey had made such a good MIM. Josh Barton was always Josh Barton. Lyptos could disappear into a part the way stars didn't, not really. Eddie watched as the actor ran his hands through his hair and cradled his head in his hands. Then Trey tapped his chest. A little double-tap over his heart.

And Eddie's gut twitched. The bile rose in his throat. "We've been morons," he said.

Shin turned to look at his partner. "Is there an explanation that goes with that insult?"

Eddie stood and grabbed his grey suit jacket in one fluid motion. "I'll explain on the way."

"Where're we going?" Shin asked as they raced to the LAPD parking lot.

"Meet me at Barton's," Eddie said as he slid into his Porsche. "But do me a solid first. Run this check on the corpse stat."

Shin nodded and got into the sedan.

When Eddie pulled his Porsche into Barton's driveway, he saw an assistant loading a pile of high-end suitcases into the star's Mercedes.

"Leaving?" Eddie asked as Josh and Petra Barton exited the house.

"We need to get away," Petra said. "This business with Trey and now Cary…it's just too much."

Eddie nodded. "Just a few details—to wrap things up." He launched into a verbal tap dance of questions for the couple that lasted about an hour.

"Are we done?" Petra said. The irritation in her tone made it clear she was anxious to get Josh out of town and away from prying eyes.

"Yeah," Eddie said as his phone pinged. He glanced down.

Shin was two minutes out. He'd attached a file. Eddie sighed. This was one time he'd wanted to be wrong.

"You said Trey Lyptos should be famous." Eddie stared at the actor with sad, disappointed eyes. "You got your wish. You will be famous. Just not for acting."

As the couple exchanged puzzled looks, a squad car pulled up. Shin exited. A second squad car right behind Shin's boxed in the actor's Mercedes.

"Mr. Lyptos," Eddie said, "You and Petra Barton need to come downtown for more questions. About the murder of Josh Barton."

"You're insane!" Petra spat. "This is Josh! Cary Giudice killed Trey."

Eddie nodded. "I wondered about Cary. She wasn't on the guest list. Did you text her on burner? You had to let her in. Why let the crazy ex-wife come to the party unless she had a role you wanted her to play? You needed somebody to take the rap in case we didn't buy the accidental OD. Cary saw what she thought was Josh out cold on the sand. She put a dermal on him. But once she left you went back and added another just to make sure. This one had a lethal dose of Ice and Spice. You knew the security system was off for the night. You didn't know Cary'd kill herself when she heard, but that only makes it more convincing."

"What are you talking about?" the actor said. "I'm Josh Barton." He held out his arm. "Scan me."

"The chip belongs to Barton," Eddie said. "Just like the chip in the corpse at the morgue read Trey Lyptos. But DNA proves otherwise. Did you swap the chips or pay somebody to remote-wipe and reprogram them?"

The actor fell silent.

Eddie nodded, noting the slight abrasion on the skin of the actor's outstretched forearm matched the one on the corpse. "That's why you staged such a public death. Barton was a star. You counted on us trusting the visuals, backed up by the swapped identity chips. And we did. For a while."

Petra sputtered on about how she was going to sue Eddie, the LAPD, and the city for slander.

Until Shin read Lyptos and Petra their rights. The blue-suiters slapped cuffs on the pair.

"You don't understand," Petra wailed. "You don't know what he was like. Josh was a shit."

"I get that," Eddie said. "But it didn't give you the right to kill him and steal his life."

Eddie knew the couple would lawyer up and deny everything, but they were going away for a long time. Suddenly the whole case and everybody in it made him feel tired and a little bit dirty.

Eddie and Shin stood there watching as blue-suiters tucked the pair into a squad car for their trip downtown.

"Lots of people will miss Josh Barton," Shin said when they were gone.

"Just...not the people who knew him." Eddie turned toward his Porsche. His lip curled.

"Case tarnish your ride?"

Eddie shrugged. They'd made the right collar, but he'd never feel quite the same way again about his Porsche or the star or himself.

"Enough to sell?" Shin punched Eddie's arm with a mock jab.

"You kidding?" The ghost of his wolfish grin flitted across Eddie's face. "Let's head to the gym, old man. You can work off that gut."

Together in Eddie's old Porsche the partners sped off into the twilight.

MANIPULATIONS

Barrie Summy

I uncross my legs, about to stand, when Dr. Cheryl addresses me from across the circle of chairs. "Tanya," she says, "could you stay for a few minutes?"

I settle back into the plastic chair. Like I have a choice. You can't say no to an authority figure in this facility, even a fairly nice one like Dr. Cheryl.

The other women file out. A few shoot me nosy glances. Some scurry past to get to lunch. A couple exit the room crying, which is par for the course after Group.

I can't think of a single reason why the therapist wants to talk to me. Unless it's about the new girl, the one who spends all day lying on her bunk. Please don't let it be that. I'm not looking for a friend. My last friend was Machelle Hayes, and that didn't end well.

"Something popped up in my Facebook feed that made me think of you," Dr. Cheryl says. She's standing in front of me.

I crane my neck, waiting for her to continue.

"An organization of mystery writers is putting together an anthology of crime short stories. You're a reader. You're always checking books out of the library. Maybe you'd like to write about your personal experience. I'll submit it, and we'll see what happens from there."

I go completely still for a second. "Really?"

Dr. Cheryl nods and pushes her glasses up on her nose. "Even if your story doesn't get chosen for the anthology, I believe it'll be helpful for you, cathartic even, to write down the details."

I ignore her psychobabble. It'll be frustrating, not cathartic. Who wants to be reminded of how their own stupidity got them boxed in?

Still, to share, in black and white, the truth of what happened? And have it published? Including my name? To get another shot at convincing people of what truly went down. That's worth something.

So, immediately following a typically unimaginative lunch, I head to the library and get situated at a desktop. I log in and begin typing. Then I hold down the delete key. Then I stare at the blank screen for a while. Then I type a little more. Then I'm back to the delete key. I honestly don't know where to start.

It's during a blank-screen phase that Dr. Cheryl shows up with unsolicited advice. "Tell the events in order. A followed by B followed by C, until you get to the end," she says. "Write about why you chose those steps and how different choices would've resulted in different outcomes."

After she leaves, I stare at the screen some more.

Behind me, the printer whirs. At the table on the other side of the computer, a woman reads under her breath, sounding out words. The back of the metal chair digs into my spine. I close my eyes and breathe in the smell of paper and books. Dr. Cheryl's got it wrong. Writing from A to B to C isn't the way to tell my story. It wouldn't convince anyone of anything. I have to start further back for people to understand. What happened seven years ago on the Saturday before Christmas actually started months before that date.

***

I used to work at Costco. Mostly on cash, but sometimes in the food court. My ex-boyfriend and I lived near Costco, within walking distance. We'd been broken up for almost a year, but neither one of us could afford to move out. So, we just kept sharing the rent. He slept on the couch. Mostly.

We lived at the Rosewood Apartments. Just to be clear, there isn't a rose anywhere near the Rosewood Apartments. The complex should be renamed the "Dirt, One Palm and Several Ugly Cypress Trees Apartments." I mean, if you're going for accuracy.

One night it was raining hard, harder than usual for Southern California. Water was streaming down my neck and my face. I passed the palm tree and was getting close to my front door. Picking my way over the uneven sidewalk with its wide cracks, I kept my eyes on my feet. The ground was slick with wet cypress needles. I was scheduled to work the next morning and didn't want to soak my only pair of shoes. And I definitely couldn't afford a sprained ankle with no health insurance and no paid sick time.

Suddenly, I slammed right into someone. My toe caught in a crack. I lost my balance. I hit the ground.

Machelle, although I didn't know her name yet, yelped. "Walk much?" she snapped, glaring down at me.

"Sorry," I said.

Why did I apologize? I could've snapped back. I mean, it was a mutual crashing, right? But I was cold and wet. My feet throbbed from standing all day, ringing up other people's purchases. I was too tired to snap. Plus, by nature, I'm not much of a snapper.

According to Machelle, that "sorry" was how she knew instantly I was the kind of person she wanted to be friends with.

We ended up going to her apartment, which was across the pathway from mine and Anthony's. She made me an exotic flowery tea, gave me makeup wipes for the mascara streaks on my face, and loaned me shoes for the next day.

Machelle's apartment was perfect, like a department store setup. Classy. The beige couch and chairs and an ottoman all matched. A picture in an actual frame hung on the wall. Her dishes were a set. Not like my place with its saggy Goodwill furniture, mismatched dishes, and a poster of Anthony's favorite rapper taped up in the living room.

After tea, I cleaned her kitchen, demonstrating my secret vinegar tip for shining up the faucet.

That's how I got in the habit of cleaning Machelle's apartment. I often picked up groceries for her, too. She got me hooked on avocados, her favorite vegetable. I mean fruit. Avocados are fruit. Machelle only reminded me of that a million times.

Anthony called me a pathetic doormat. "If she told you to jump off the Coronado Bridge, you'd do it," he'd say.

But I didn't see it that way. For me, it was all about friendship. Cleaning Machelle's apartment and running errands for her proved we were friends. And I hadn't had many of those in life. Friends want to do things for each other is how I explained it to Anthony. He shrugged. "Whatever gets you through the night, Tanya."

Anyway, it wasn't all one-sided. Machelle gave me stuff. Like her hand-me-downs. That got me dressing like her in tighter jeans and crop tops and high heels. And she gave me shower gel from Bath and Body Works. We both smelled the same, sweet and citrusy. One day, she unhooked a framed print of yellow flowers in a vase from her wall and handed it to me. I nailed it up in place of Anthony's poster.

Teralyn, who lived with her aunt next door to Machelle and sometimes hung out with us, noticed right away how I was changing. "What are you?" Teralyn said. "A mini-Machelle?"

I didn't bother answering. Teralyn wouldn't recognize friendship if it poked her in the eye. She worked at Costco with me. Before Costco, we attended the same high school. We never discussed it, but we were both losers on subsidized lunches. One spring, the PTA bought me a speedo, so I could join the swim team. For the fall of junior year, Teralyn and her dad and her little brother lived in their car. Teralyn's dad drank too much. My mom liked meth.

Machelle started inviting me over in the evenings. Her boyfriend, Kaden, was planning to move in soon, but hadn't yet. He worked four to midnight at Local Brews, a craft beer and burger joint, and Machelle got lonely. I was happy to get out of my apartment. Most nights, Anthony and his buddies played video games and smoked weed in front of our TV.

Machelle did my makeup and showed me how to straight-iron my hair. I gave her pedicures, and she swore they were better than any she'd gotten at a nail salon. We baked cookies and drank wine. I was living those high school bestie times I never had.

Lucky for Machelle, I was more the quiet, introverted, listener type. Because that girl could monologue for hours. She'd chat a little about her job at the water district and a little about other Rosewood Apartment tenants. But her two main topics of choice were the news and Kaden.

Machelle was a huge news junkie and couldn't believe I wasn't up on everything. She was always trying to educate me into seeing things her way.

And then there was Kaden. Machelle was so in love with him, her eyes glassed over just saying his name. Those two made the perfect couple. Sometimes, I'd tell Machelle about the hero in the romance novel I was reading. We'd figure out how he measured up to Kaden. We decided Kaden was identical to Jamie Fraser from Outlander. How romantic was that?

Weird as it sounds, I was falling in love with Machelle and Kaden. More like I was falling in love with the idea of their relationship. When he bought her flowers for their six-month anniversary, my heart swelled up. When he complimented her new highlights, it was like he complimented my hair, too. When he hugged her after her boss yelled at her for being late again, I was consoled.

Of course, I knew it wasn't my relationship. I was well aware of that. I wasn't an idiot. But I felt protective of them.

Once, when Teralyn and I were working the Costco food court together, she asked me why I was dragging around and taking forever to restock the condiments at the hotdog bar.

"Is it cramps?" she asked. "I got Advil in my purse."

"Machelle and Kaden are fighting," I said, blinking back tears. "It's just getting me down, I guess."

Teralyn raised her thick, painted-on eyebrows. "Is anyone fighting with you personally? Machelle? Kaden? Anthony? Our moron boss?"

"No," I answered, hugging a huge jar of mustard to my chest.

She stared unblinking at me like I was a bug under a microscope. Finally, she shook her head. "Tanya, you're too softhearted for your own good. Also, you're weirder than I realized. Machelle and Kaden's relationship—which isn't yours, by the way—won't go the distance. Kaden will get tired of Machelle. The way every guy does once he realizes Machelle's only interested in one person." Teralyn paused. "And that person is Machelle."

Poor Teralyn, I thought, already so cynical about love. No wonder she never has a boyfriend.

One evening, I was sitting in Machelle's kitchen. We were drinking white wine from actual wine glasses. The wine was cold and sweet and French.

"Remember that cop last spring in Ohio who accidentally got a few granules of fentanyl on his skin and almost died?" Machelle asked. She was always doing that, quizzing me about news stories from before.

"Vaguely," I replied. Fiction stuck more in my memory than facts.

Machelle frowned. "How about the mass shooting in Vegas? At the country-music concert with Jason Aldean? The gunman shot at people from his Mandalay Bay hotel window?" she said. "Surely you remember that. It was only the deadliest mass shooting by an individual in the history of our country."

"Yeah, I remember that." I nodded, grateful I really did remember something.

"The Vegas massacre happened around the same time as the Ohio cop almost dying of fentanyl." Machelle tilted her wine glass toward me.

I topped it off. "Okay," I said.

"Guess who's selling fentanyl in our complex?" Machelle said.

"Dougie?" I asked. It was a logical guess. Dougie was our local dealer.

"Exactly. And I told him about the Ohio story." Machelle swirled her wine. "About how the cop merely brushed a few specks of powder off his uniform with his bare hand. The powder turned out to be fentanyl, and it got absorbed into the cop's system through his skin. Then he overdosed. It took four shots of Narcan to save his life."

"Very scary," I said.

"Dougie thanked me and said now that he knows, he'll wear gloves when he's handling fentanyl." Machelle narrowed her eyes at me. "See why it's important to stay current on the news?"

"Sure thing," I said, and sipped more wine.

"I'm serious, Tanya," Machelle said.

"I know." And that's when I decided to start writing the news stories on notecards and reading them over before going to Machelle's. Then I wouldn't get tripped up when she questioned me. And my stomach wouldn't clench, waiting for her to frown and stare at me like I was the dumbest friend she ever had.

Machelle got quiet, running her index finger up and down the stem of her glass.

"I really do get it," I repeated.

"I believe you." She stayed quiet.

"Is something wrong?" I asked.

She swigged a big mouthful of wine and swallowed. "It's Kaden. I feel so awful for him. He's working way too much, and it's really getting to him."

"That's too bad," I said, meaning it.

"We have to make my holiday party the best ever. To lift Kaden's spirits." She raised her glass. "Deal?"

"Deal," I said, clinking with her.

We jumped into making lists for food and decorations. We invited more people. It would be the biggest, funnest, rockingest holiday party ever held at the Rosewood Apartments.

A couple of weeks later, the Saturday morning of the party, Teralyn and I were at Machelle's, helping her get ready.

I'd just finished scrubbing the toilet when Machelle called out from the kitchen. "Tanya! Teralyn!"

I scooped up my supplies and jogged down the hall. I poked my head into the living room where Teralyn was bent over, plumber's crack showing, vacuuming under the couch.

"Teralyn," I shouted over the roar. "Machelle wants us in the kitchen."

She switched off the vacuum. "Well, if Her Highness has spoken," Teralyn muttered sarcastically.

Machelle was leaning against the stove, staring at her phone screen. "I am beyond bummed. Chloe's bailing tonight."

"Who's Chloe?" I peeled off the disposable plastic gloves I always wore when I cleaned Machelle's bathroom and dropped them in the trash.

Machelle rolled her eyes. "Come on, Tanya. Do you have any memory?"

"Kinda tall. Dark hair. Lives on the other side of the complex. Works at the mall," Teralyn said, hiking up her jeans.

Still didn't ring a bell with me, but I didn't say anything.

"Why's she ditching at the last minute?" Teralyn asked.

Machelle scrolled on her phone. It took a few tries. She

had the longest acrylic nails in the world. Very cute, but they got in the way of everything, which is why Teralyn and I were doing the bulk of the party work.

"How should I know?" Machelle said, her face blotchy with annoyance. "She's not answering my texts. We have to make her come. She was bringing her guitar and about twenty people from the west side. The party'll be a disaster of boredom without her. Kaden will hate it. She has to come."

The three of us stood there in silence. I was scrutinizing the kitchen floor, deciding to skip washing it. After all, it was only going to get dirty again during the party.

"Chloe needs to understand how important her presence is tonight," Machelle said.

"You could walk over to her apartment," Teralyn suggested, "and tell her how much you're counting on her."

Machelle briefly closed her eyes. "You know what?" she said, smiling at Teralyn. "That is a brilliant idea."

Teralyn beamed. "Yeah, well, you're welcome."

"I'll write her a personal invitation, and Tanya can take it over."

"What? No." I shook my head so fast the floor blurred. "I don't even know her. No, no, no."

"I'll write her apartment number on the envelope." Machelle opened a drawer and pulled out a pen and a card.

"Seriously. Why me?" I said. "It's your party, Machelle. You should go."

"You can handle it, Tanya," Teralyn said. Turning her back on Machelle, she mouthed at me, "Take one for the team."

"You're more persuasive," Machelle said, "because you're completely non-threatening."

The next thing I knew I was pushed, literally pushed, out Machelle's front door.

I stood on the sidewalk. I could just go home. Throw the card in the trash. Ditch the party myself.

Machelle banged on the window.

I started walking. Sometimes it felt like Machelle wound me up like a toy just to watch me spin.

The complex is divided in half by Magnolia Street. The east side and the west side are even in different cities, Lakewood and Corona. East and west people don't mix and mingle too often. Machelle's holiday party was an exception.

At Magnolia Street, I pushed the crosswalk button. It was a typical December day. The sun was shining, but the breeze was cool. I zipped up my hoodie. The dog in the corner apartment barked whenever a car whizzed by. There was a greasy, fast-food smell from the nearby Taco Bell.

The pedestrian light flashed, and I set out across the road, leaving Lakewood and entering Corona.

In my kangaroo pocket, my phone vibrated with a call from Machelle.

"Found her apartment yet?" she asked.

"No," I said. "I just crossed Magnolia."

"Okay." Machelle hung up.

I took the first pathway, wending my way into the interior of the west side.

I stopped and peered around to get my bearings. It was different over here. The apartment numbers were bigger and easier to spot. There were several palms, not just one, and no ugly cypress trees. Containers of sweet-smelling flowers lined the walkways.

It didn't take long to find Chloe's apartment. Fourteen A was on the second floor. I stood by a palm tree, fingering Machelle's card.

My phone vibrated again.

"Where are you?" Machelle asked.

"Near her apartment," I said. "But I really don't want to do this."

Machelle yakked at me for a few minutes. The upshot was she wanted Chloe at the party, and I didn't have a choice.

"You'll be fine," she said and hung up.

Could I dash up the stairs, drop the card on the mat, knock the door and dash down? Did I even have to talk to Chloe?

Chloe's apartment door opened.

Kaden stepped out.

I flattened myself against the bumpy palm trunk.

Chloe stepped out. She slid her cell phone into her pocket.

They kissed. A very long kiss.

My stomach dropped to the dirt I was standing on. My legs turned to jelly. My heart shattered into pieces.

They kissed again before Chloe backed into her apartment and shut the door. Kaden took the stairs two at a time, then ran along the path and out of view.

Still squished against the palm, I waited till my legs were strong enough for walking. My heart was never going to mend. Then I followed the path to Magnolia Street and crossed back to my side of the complex.

When I got to my apartment, I unlocked the door and fell in.

"What's with Machelle's favorite minion?" Anthony asked from the entryway to the kitchen. "Worn to the bone with all the party prep?"

"I saw Kaden and a girl named Chloe kissing." The words came out jerky and raw.

"Old news," Anthony said. "He's been seeing her for a couple of months."

"What?" My legs went wobbly again, and I slumped against the wall. "Why?"

"Why not? If he can get away with it, any guy's going to do it." Anthony dug in his front jeans pocket. "I'm surprised Machelle hasn't figured it out."

"Well, she hasn't. She would've told me." She definitely would've told me if Kaden was cheating on us. More than anything in the world, Machelle hated a cheater. That's what her dad was, and it ruined her childhood.

Anthony shrugged and held out some crumpled bills. "Run

up to Dougie's for me?"

On autopilot, I took the money and went back out and upstairs to Dougie's apartment.

Standing on his stoop, my brain all fuzzy and slow moving, I thought of the fentanyl story. I could see the exact notecard with my careful printing. Machelle brought up that story several times. Each time, after I got home from her apartment, I'd jot down the little bit of extra information she'd added. I could hear her voice in my head, relaying her conversation with Dougie about wearing gloves. Then, she was quizzing me on how little fentanyl it took to knock out the cop, how he'd picked up the fentanyl granules during a routine traffic stop, how a disgruntled employee wiped fentanyl on his boss after not getting promoted. Lots of details. I memorized them all.

The prosecutor made it sound like I sat down with an Excel spreadsheet and planned out the whole thing. He kept repeating "premeditated." Not true. It started as a whisper of an idea in a shell-shocked brain in a body with a broken heart.

The party was in full swing when Anthony and I arrived.

I felt Machelle's twinge of annoyance when she opened the door to us. She's into punctuality. But she recovered quickly, smiled and waved us in with big arm movements.

"Is that Chloe?" Anthony tilted his head toward the kitchen.

That was when I heard guitar music.

"Yes! Chloe and her friends are here," Machelle practically sang.

Anthony wandered off, in search of beer.

Machelle hugged me. "Thank you for persuading Chloe. You're the best, best friend."

Which, of course, I wasn't. The card was in my trash. But I leaned into the hug. I didn't tell her about Kaden or explain that I didn't know why Chloe had changed her mind about skipping the party. I let it all ride, not wanting to wreck the moment.

Machelle squealed.

Kaden had snuck up behind her and grabbed her around the waist.

Squeezing by them, and avoiding Kaden's eyes, I went to the kitchen and poured myself a shot of vodka.

Chloe was strumming "Rudolph the Red-Nosed Reindeer." She had green glitter in her hair to match her green sparkly top. People, including Teralyn, were singing along. Everyone looked festive and happy.

I felt nauseous.

Dark, angry thoughts of Kaden and his cheating swirled inside me. He was cheating on Machelle. He was cheating on Chloe. He was cheating on me.

I slammed more vodka shots.

Over the course of the evening, I passed Kaden several times. In the living room. In the hall. In the kitchen. I could see myself pulling on a plastic glove and swiping fentanyl granules on his arm or maybe the back of his neck.

Machelle yanked me into the bathroom. "What's your problem?" she said. "You're scowling at everyone."

"I hate Kaden," I slurred. "Take this or I might actually end up killing him." I handed her the small packet of fentanyl.

Machelle pocketed it. "You really are the best best friend." Her finger in the small of my back, she nudged me toward the sound of the guitar. "Go listen to some music." Her acrylic nail was sharp.

Chloe and her entourage had migrated to the living room. She was sitting on the ottoman. I stood behind her, swaying and unsteady. I started singing.

Kaden walked over and handed me a bottle of water. "From Machelle. So you don't have a headache tomorrow."

Machelle joined us. She stood on the other side of Kaden.

And then I saw her right hand. She was wearing a disposable glove. The tip of the index finger was coated in white powder. With a deft movement, she rubbed Kaden's neck.

Within seconds he was passed out on the floor.

"I told him to slow down with the shots," Machelle said, rolling her eyes in a boyfriends-never-listen kind of way. "Let's get him into the bedroom."

Chloe briefly lifted a hand from strumming to give Machelle a thumb's up.

A couple of the guys maneuvered Kaden down the hall.

Of course, the fentanyl showed up on the autopsy. Dougie told the police about me buying it from him right before the party. Lots of people remembered me angry and upset that night, giving Kaden the stink eye. Machelle told the detectives I had an unrequited crush on Kaden. She said it'd been a huge blow to me to learn he was moving in with her. Teralyn told the detectives I'd always been weird, all the way back to high school. The biggest nail in my coffin was the disposable glove with fentanyl on the outside and my DNA on the inside. The detectives actually laughed when I explained how Machelle worked that. With the glove she wore to kill Kaden, she swiped fentanyl on the glove I'd worn to clean her bathroom the morning of the party. Then she hid my glove back in her kitchen trash for the police to find. She must've disposed of her glove somewhere away from her apartment. Maybe Chloe got rid of it.

No one believed my side of the story. Not the detectives or my pro bono lawyer or the judge or the jury.

Dr. Cheryl asks me to stay after Group again. "I read your story, Tanya. I'll be honest." She sighs. "I'm disappointed. I thought you'd made more headway with accepting responsibility."

I open my mouth to launch into how the short story was my experience, my exact experience.

"There's no ownership, no remorse on your part. With Group and with our individuals, I really thought you were further along. I guess I was wrong," Dr. Cheryl says, shaking her head sadly.

My heart flutters like a panicky bird is trapped in my chest. What was I thinking, writing my story the way it transpired? What will happen when I'm up for parole? Dr. Cheryl won't go to bat for me. That's what'll happen. But I want out. I want early parole. It's what keeps me going. I hate my locked-up life.

"Dr. Cheryl," I say slowly, swallowing my truth, staring at my canvas slip-on shoes. "I feel awful about what I did. Truly awful. No one feels more remorse than me." I pause, searching for the words that'll do the trick. "And you called it. Writing the story was cathartic. It's like an emotional weight has been lifted from me. I feel like I can stand up straight now. And face the world.

"The thing is, I had to write my story as fiction. I had to. To give it a better chance of getting in the anthology. And I think it works. I might even have a talent for creative writing. Me having a talent for something? That's a first."

I take a deep breath and carry on. "I made up how Machelle kept texting me that afternoon, timing it right with Chloe so I'd see her and Kaden kiss. And how Machelle had Kaden deliver a bottle of water to me so he'd be standing by me when he passed out. And then there was the crazy, convoluted explanation of how my DNA ended up inside a glove with fentanyl on the outside."

I stop talking. I've run out of things to say. My heart throws itself against my ribcage.

There's silence.

Finally, I look up.

Dr. Cheryl is staring at me, her eyes glistening behind her glasses. "I'm proud of you, Tanya. You got it all figured out."

THUMBING THE DIVE

Lauren Avenius

As he stepped off the plane at Cancun International, the heat hit him like a wall. He squinted against the midday sun. It was noon, and the tropical light glittered on the tarmac, still wet from a passing storm. Steam rose from every surface and glowed in the yellow light. *It looks like a fucking Disney movie*, James thought.

He was lumbering, in a fog, and his head ached. There was a heaviness in his movements. In the bathroom back at John Wayne Airport, just before boarding his flight, he had cracked a small vial and taken in deeply the one thing he knew would help him take a flight like this, a case like this—what they called "asset collection." But his head still wasn't in the game, and he knew it.

He didn't call it a job—they were never jobs. Rob, who had gotten him into the business, would never use that word. *Job.* It was too gauche. No, it was accounts, clients, portfolios. Rob had the healthy tan of a man accustomed to outdoor sports all his life—yachting, tennis, golf—but he never did anything that resembled work. "A job," Rob said, "is something a prostitute does for money, and it usually involves hands, mouth, or both if she's any good."

James rubbed his face. Damn, it was bright. And hot. His head throbbed and his hands were sweating—he was beginning to think he had taken too much. It was going to be a hard few days.

He slid his bag over his shoulder and walked across the tarmac to customs.

The night before, at the weekly poker game, Rob had pulled James aside. He was outside on the patio of Rob's beach house, smoking a cigarette and watching the waves, when Rob came up to him. He was with another guy James didn't know. He nodded to James, who stubbed out his cigarette and followed Rob inside. He could tell when they were taking a client.

"Mike, this is Jimmy, the guy I was telling you about. Very discreet." Rob emphasized discreet in a way that James knew was meant for him. He nodded and extended his hand.

"Ah, great to meet you." Mike said, smiling eagerly. He was tall and blond, but paunchier and paler than the rest of the guys. He looked like he might actually work.

"So, Jimmy, Mike has a little situation that I think you could really help him with," Rob said. "It'd be a special favor to me." They had never taken on "special favors" or discussed clients at poker night before. It gave things a tense air, almost surreal. Here was Rob walking him through a client intro, prepping the details, but everyone was in Tommy Bahama shirts holding mixed drinks while The Eagles's "Take It Easy" was playing in the background. It made James feel like they were in an episode of *Miami Vice* or something.

"This is her," Mike said, handing a picture to James. "It's my daughter, she's gone missing. She went down to Cancun for some damned scuba trip, and she disappeared." Mike continued about his daughter's trip and her friends, the hotel and the flights, where and when she was supposed to have checked in and didn't, but James kept holding the picture. He was haunted by it. Her wavy blonde hair, her grayish-blue eyes, there was something in the smile that hit him. She was twenty-one but looked like she could have been anywhere from fifteen to thirty, one of those beautiful girls who looks both endlessly young and somehow ageless. And her smile. Happy and bright, but so vulnerable, like her eyes were reaching out to you.

James put down the picture and listened as Mike explained the situation—why they weren't getting the authorities involved, high-profile clientele, bad press. Things James had heard before. It was usually the case; affairs and bad loans, just the whiff of bad luck and investors started fleeing. Men like this traded on their names and histories, and if yours was tainted, that was the end.

Later, walking out to their cars, Rob caught up with James and threw his arm around his shoulders. "So head down there, take a look and see what you find. Chances are this girl's just shacked up with some surfer, smoking pot and doing yoga. But I'd like to get this taken care of soon, if you know what I mean."

"*Buenos dias*, Senior Tanner, and welcome to Secrets Maroma. How long will you be staying with us?"

"Two days." James's Spanish was good enough that he didn't need the English concierge, but he wanted to seem like a tourist and tourists don't speak Spanish, at least not in these types of resorts.

He squinted across the lobby—a white marbled expanse that opened seamlessly onto the resort's miles-long pool, cabanas stretching as far as he could see, straight out to Maroma's famed private beach. Like a sexy person parking lot for the extravagantly wealthy, he thought. Just then, two girls in floral tunics and teal bikinis walked barefoot across the white stone lobby toward the pool.

"I want to go scuba diving while I'm here. Do you have

rentals on site?" he asked, still watching the girls.

The concierge smiled appreciatively. "*Jyes*, of course." The concierge took in appreciatively James's small bag, casual clothing, and apparent singleness, and pushed forward a few brochures highlighting the spa and "romantic" events planned. "We also have many services for the single traveler."

"Good to know." He went up to his room, dropped off his bag, and changed into khaki cargo shorts and a faded red T. He pocketed some cash, all dollars—everywhere in Latin America accepts dollars—along with his room key, a small utility knife, and a lighter. He took a deep breath and one last look at Emma's picture before walking out toward the pool.

He got into the business not by accident, but not deliberately either. He had been playing a pickup match at the Newport Beach Tennis Club with a man he'd just met. James beat him, but the man didn't seem to mind. He said James seemed like a fun guy, and when he found out he played poker, too, well that cinched it. He invited him to his private table, a small game held at a local fund manager's house, "a few high rollers and a couple whales," and told him to come with an appetite and two thousand in cash for the buy-in.

At the house, James was well liked immediately. He held his cards close to his chest, they said. And read them all like books. "You're seeing through me like pink panties through a white dress," they all laughed. They liked him in an easy, natural way, and he liked being with them, even though he was younger than most of their kids, or wives for that matter, if they had them, which most didn't, or seemed to be between. But they didn't talk much about that, either. They drank beer and someone broke out an expensive Scotch, and they smoked cigars at the table and cigarettes outside.

On the patio, one of them came up to him, sipping slowly from two fingers of the expensive Scotch. "I like how you handled yourself in there. Guy your age, comes to a table with a bunch of men he doesn't know, a place he's never been, shows up with a billfold and keen eye, and suddenly you're running the room. That's a skill, you know. To read a man's hand is one thing. But to win on it, that's another."

James didn't respond; he knew better than to think he was being complimented. So instead he brought his cigarette to his mouth and squinted against the glow, letting the silence and the smoke say it instead. He knew when he was being tuned up, but he was interested in the pitch. This man had played fewer hands, but the ones he did he won well. He was confident, laughed, but kept himself under the radar. "So, what do you do?" James asked, after a pause.

This was the right question, the lead-in. The Two-Fingered Scotch swirled in his drink, and said, "Maybe something you could do, too." And that was how it started—a tennis match and a poker game.

Down at the pool James looked for the two blondes in tunics. They were lying in lounge chairs, laughing and drinking. One was applying suntan lotion while the other was pulling magazines from her bag. He stopped by the bar, ordered a Dos Equis, and walked toward them.

"I'm James."

"I'm Katie, and this is Kaitlyn," lotion-girl said. "And no, we're not related." She giggled. It was only noon, but they already looked drunk. He guessed they were twenty-three.

His head throbbed. He wanted to be back in the air-conditioned room, finishing off another vial, not chasing down some beach bunny in Mexico. But he smiled broadly, convincingly, all the same, and the two blondes in tunics smiled back sweetly.

***

An hour later, Katie and Kaitlyn and James were driving down the beach, headed toward a rental shack Katie knew. She had met the guy in the hotel bar, and after a few drinks he had given her his number and the promise of a discount.

"Hola, hola, hola," Katie said, walking in the way young hot girls do—never questioning whether she'll be remembered.

"Hey, Kat-TEE," said an overly tanned, underly sober twenty-something American. He looked at James, sizing him up. "Hey man, I'm Tristan. Cool to meet you." He slapped James a handshake. "So what's the deal, girl? Are we gonna get wet?"

James took in the scuba shack. He assumed that within one week, thousands of people might come to this stretch of beach alone. Playa is the top tourist destination in Mexico—the equivalent of the entire population of Newport Beach traveling through the Cancun Airport every day. But standing there, James knew he had stumbled into the right spot. He looked at Tristan, and just knew he had met Emma. Probably bought her a drink in the same bar where he had met Katie. James looked at his two tunic-wearing blondes like they were tiny, sexy, little angels. He rubbed his eyes, licked his lips, and pulled out his lighter, flicking it absent-mindedly while Katie let Tristan hit on her.

"So James wants to learn to scuba," Katie said, pulling at her bikini strings.

"Sorry, dude, last boat already left. But tomorrow, we have boats leaving every two hours. Just give us an hour to get you hooked up, cool?"

"Yeah, cool, tomorrow." James flicked his lighter again.

"So, if we're not diving, what are we up to now, girls? Pretty sure you owe me a drink, Katie."

They continued a back and forth of jokes and stories James only pretended to listen to, but in the end, it was decided that they would all go to a bar just down the sand from the rental shack. It was a tourist trap shanty bar, complete with fishing nets and fake starfish hanging from the ceiling.

After a few beers and the girls' second trip to the jukebox, Tristan turned to James. "You ever been diving before?"

"No."

"You never forget your first," he said, mostly non-ironically. "So why take it up now?"

James loved these guys, guys who couldn't stand being quiet, who would say anything just to have something said. He leaned forward, closer to Tristan, and pulled out his phone.

"My friend Emma told me about it. Sent me all these pictures and told me I had to come." He showed the pictures to Tristan, of her in a bikini at the beach that he had pulled from her Facebook page.

"Dude, her? You know that chick?" He looked at James with new appreciation and tipped his beer in approval.

"Yeah. Why, you know her?"

"Oh, yeah. A girl like that does not go *unnoticed.* We spent a bit of time together. But she never mentioned diving. She was on a totally different trip, man. If you know what I mean."

James pulled his lighter from his pocket and flicked it. "No, I don't know what you mean."

"Sure, you do, man. You definitely do." At this point, the girls were back, fresh from their adventure at the jukebox, and eager for the boys' attention. Their drunken youthful energy cut into Tristan's words like a commercial break. Tristan slapped James on the arm, "But don't you worry, I've got what you need."

"Let's go swimming," one of the girls said.

"I've got a better idea. Let's head back to my place. I'll grill up some food, we'll have some more drinks, and you girls can dive from the deck right into the crystal blue. We'll have ourselves a paaart-*tay.*" He winked at James. There was something very Matthew McConaughey about him. James couldn't decide whether it was the hint of a southern accent, or knowing he was on the right trail—or maybe it was the promise of getting "what he needs" —but he started liking Tristan.

***

Tristan lived in a three-bedroom condo on the water. The back opened up to the ocean, the deck blending into the living room. There were a few people already there, sitting on the couches smoking and drinking. More people like Tristan, young and white with sun-bleached hair and the types of tans that took years to build and would take years to fade. James had seen them in countries all over the world, shiftless and aimless, and somehow always laughing, washing up on shores in beach towns just like this, gathering in rooms just like this, before moving on again. Like the foam the waves wash up on shore, just back and forth to a rhythm and current that nothing else seems caught up in.

Tristan got the girls cold beers and then nodded James down a hallway. He opened the door to a small room, where three guys were sitting in the muted light. The smell was what hit him first. Sweet and acrid, with a tinge of something he didn't know. Tristan and the three exchanged nods and hand slaps, then one of them handed Tristan a small glass pipe. He took a hit and, still holding it in, passed it to James.

"What's this?" James asked. But no one responded. Tristan just nodded an encouraging *yes* and pushed it at him again. James took a hit. It came on instantaneously and hard. His head felt unhinged, like a pin had been pulled and it was free to roll and float up, as if it had just been waiting for a door to open and to rollercoaster out of his skull.

"Hey, man, you with us?" Tristan's voice came to him like an eel swimming in water.

"That's good stuff," James said. The three other guys laughed. "Man, I wish Emma had mentioned this instead. This is way better than diving."

"Hey, Deven, this guy is friends with Emma. You remember her, right? That crazy blonde chick from Cali, blew through here like what, four or five days ago? She sent him down here man, and he randomly ends up at my shop. Can you believe that shit?" Tristan was laughing.

"That's crazy," Deven said. "But man, she was crazy. She took half my stash when she left. She was hot, though." Deven looked at James for a second, like maybe he would ask him to pay for it, but then decided against it. That wasn't the code here. Here, a hot girl steals your stuff, you just accept it as something hot chicks do. No one else has to be taken up for it.

"So she was staying here? I thought she was at Maroma, I mean that's where she told me to stay," James said.

"Yeah, that hotel." They all laughed.

"What? What am I missing?"

"Man, you notice all the hottest talent is hanging out by that pool? But it's nowhere near anything, and it's not cheap, either, bro."

"Okay, so?"

"So, the hotel makes it worth their while to hang out there. I mean, some of these girls were even *invited* by the hotel to be there." Deven took another hit. "Like, they get flown out from the States to stay a few days. It's nutso, girls you wouldn't expect. Not your normal pros, but like straight up the girls next door, literally."

"Emma was mixed up in that?" James asked, trying not to seem too eager.

"I don't know, man, but she was mixed up in something," Tristan said. He passed the pipe back to Deven and the other two guys, neither of whom had done anything more than laugh since James had sat down.

"That's crazy, I didn't think Emma was the type." James felt obvious, like he was fishing.

"Then you didn't know her very well," Tristan said, standing up. "Come on, I can hear those girls calling for us." James could hear the girls squeal from the other room, and a few seconds later, the splashing and laughing as they jumped into the ocean. It was nearing sunset, and the birds were making themselves known outside. He was tempted to stay, have a little more of whatever it was they were passing around, maybe drink a cold beer and watch the girls swim. But more than anything he wanted to get this done. Something about this whole thing made him itch.

As he got up to leave, Deven stopped him. "Hey man, that Emma chick, she was trouble. I saw her down at this bar over on Calle Benito like two days ago, way on the other side of town. She had no reason being there, you know? If you're, like, with this chick, I'd be careful."

"Was she with anybody when you saw her?" James asked. He still felt heavy underwater.

Deven paused. Bit his lip. "Yeah, like a local-looking guy. Tattoo on his arm of a flamingo smoking a cigarette. Sounds dumb but not the type of guy you want to mess with." Deven gave James a knowing look. A bro looking after a bro, thought James. "I'm just saying, be careful. She said she met him at the hotel but that was obviously bullshit."

"Thanks. So much for scuba, I guess."

"Fuck scuba," Deven said.

It was after dark when he got back to the hotel. He went straight to the pool bar and ordered a tequila, sucked the lime and grimaced. He looked around and saw Kaitlyn walking up from the patio.

"I thought you were staying for barbecue?"

"Oh, yeah, I promised I'd be here tonight. Katie's still there, though." She seemed nervous.

"What do you mean 'be here,'" he asked.

"You know, just, like, um." She stopped talking and looked up at James, her clear blue eyes suddenly sharp. "You know, be here."

"Are you meeting someone?" He should have been asking about Emma, but he was feeling confused. Maybe he was still a little too high from Tristan's stash. He felt like he had been pulled down a slow current, sucked in a riptide.

She exhaled loudly, softly. "Oh, no one in particular, you know, just hanging out here and seeing who wants company."

"Wait, are you—"

"No, come on, it's not like that." She shifted in her seat. "You know, just hang out at the bar, and make nice. If I meet someone and we want to spend more time together or whatever that's completely on me, it's not like we are expected to sleep with anyone. Just, you know, look pretty and be nice. That's the deal. And I'm always pretty and always nice, so," she said in a self-conscious half-mocking way. But there was something else in it.

"Is someone paying you to be here?"

"It's not like I'm a prostitute. It's just, like, places like this just want to be sure that there are people around, so it's worth it to them to have me or, you know, girls like me here. It's nothing, it's just like, people set this up," she said, wide eyes scrolling the bar. She was watching for someone. *God, she looks young*, James thought.

"How many other girls like you are here? Is Katie one?" But before she could answer he pulled out his phone and showed it to her. "Was she one of them?"

"Why do you have a picture of Emma on your phone?"

"She's a friend of mine," James said, pocketing the phone. "I'm looking for her."

"I don't understand..." Kaitlyn was starting to get confused, agitated. James grabbed her by the elbow and ushered her from the bar.

"I'm trying to find Emma, Kaitlyn. No one has heard from her. Do you know where she is? Seen her around the last few days?" They were outside now, standing near the pool. Kaitlyn's shirt flapped in the breeze and she shuddered with a chill. She tugged to free her arm, but he held firm.

"Emma was here, but she left a few days ago."

"Where did she go? Why did she leave?" James was tempted to light a cigarette, but he was worried that if he took his hand off Kaitlyn she would slip away. She seemed skittish, like a startled horse.

"Emma was acting crazy, picking fights with the guests, not like *with the program,* you know? And I don't know if they asked her to leave or if she left on her own, but next day she was gone."

"Did she go with anyone?"

She stopped, sighed. Stared at him. "Yeah, she did. But not one of the guests. Some, like, *other*-looking guy. Listen, she was out of control. It's not as if these people are our bosses, but that's not why they bring us here. We're supposed to be nice. I really need to get back into the bar. I'm sorry."

The wind had picked up, blowing heavy over the beach and across the pool, and as she backed slowly away from him, it seemed like the wind had picked her up and blown her away. He let her go.

He was trying to light a cigarette. He didn't have his lighter, only matches from the bar, but they were weak and couldn't hold a flame. After the third attempt, he swore, threw the matchbook on the table, and pocketed the cigarette. The music was loud, but distant. There was a jukebox in the far corner of the bar, crooning some old Mexican tune he remembered hearing a long time ago, maybe as a kid, but it could barely be heard over the din of clanging glasses and hushed talking. The light was dim, and the bar had red Christmas lights behind the shelves, illuminating bottles of top-shelf alcohol, but he knew places like this, and he knew that "top shelf" was just less watered-down versions of bottom shelf.

He drummed his fingers on the table, picked up his glass and took a sip. He thought about trying to light another cigarette, even picked up the matchbook, spinning it between his thumb and forefinger. He was watching the bartender, who was busy wiping away imaginary stains, prepping endlessly for the customers that would, most likely, never show. It was the type of place where a slow night was every night.

He felt a dull ache growing behind his eyes. He bent his head and rubbed his eyes, pressing hard into the soft tissue until light formed stars behind his lids.

He was beginning to reconsider.

The bartender at Maroma said he remembered that tattoo, the one with the flamingo, and said a guy like that came to the hotel sometimes. He said he remembered Emma, and maybe this guy was there when she was there, but he couldn't be sure. But he did know that that guy, and all the guys like him, wound up at a bar downtown. He wrote the address and the cross streets on a cocktail napkin and went on pouring drinks. James took the address and a cab and a seat in the corner and had been here since, waiting.

His head pounded. He was rethinking everything. Including Emma. What was a girl like that doing out here?

He could go back to the hotel, he thought, and play cards at the casino, maybe meet a girl with a pink umbrella in her drink. He could talk to a girl like that, maybe take her to dinner, maybe more. He could pretend that he really was just a guy on vacation and forget everything about this case. He could do that and wait to find his man, when he didn't have bad music playing and red lights behind the bar. When he didn't care about lighting a cigarette.

He thought about doing all these things, but when he looked up, he forgot them. Standing at the bar was a caramel-skinned girl, maybe eighteen, maybe younger, with bare shoulders and a pink and purple dress. She was stirring the ice in her drink but not waiting for the bartender to refill it. She was slender and her dress hung on her still-forming curves, the fabric rustling softly when she moved. He sipped his drink and watched her.

He didn't like prostitutes, had never liked prostitutes, and she was no different. But she was young and tender, and nervous in a way that made him forget the hardness of the women in her trade. When she turned her head, staring toward the door, her dark hair fell down her back, heavy, revealing a small and fresh cigarette burn just above her shoulder. He stared intently at the burn, the skin still scabbing, and looked to the door where she was looking.

A moment later a man walked in, took a seat in the corner by himself, and lit a cigarette. She tensed, nodded to him, and took a tentative sip from her drink. James sat up straight, replaced his glass on the table, and considered the man with the cigarette.

He considered them both. Her skin, soft like dough; how easily she would bruise and cry out. He thought about Emma and Katie and Kaitlyn, barely older than she. How safe and sheltered they seemed, how like from a different world, but really just a short cab ride away from this.

He looked at the man with the cigarette, and back at her, and thought of her young face, how back in Orange County she'd be shopping or thinking about college. She couldn't have been more than eighteen, seventeen maybe. A woman in these parts, but still just a girl.

That picture of Emma haunted him, that smile. He pictured that smile here, in this bar. In the glow of this tacky red light.

A moment later he stood up, walked to the girl in the purple and pink dress, and with his hand on the small of her back whispered in her ear.

"Eres muy linda."

She looked up. "*¿Estás sola? ¿Haga quiere a una amiga?*" she said. She gave him a wan smile, shaking slightly. He could see she was nervous. He leaned in closer, the back of his hand grazing her shoulders.

"Tell your man to meet me outside." He took her glass from her hand, put it on the bar, and motioned to the bartender to refill it.

He walked past the jukebox and out the back door into the alley. Outside, he took off his watch and ring, the turquoise one he always wore, and put them in his pocket. He could hear movement on the other side of the door, and he placed himself two steps to the right of the opening.

There was a bottle on the ground by his feet and as the door opened, he picked it up, tossed it in his hands, then threw it at the open door. It exploded against the wall inches from the cigarette man's face. The man closed his eyes, startled, and James took his opportunity. He threw a right hook, connecting just above the jaw. The girl screamed. James grabbed him by the collar and pulled him close, lifting him slightly, and with his forehead broke the man's nose. The cigarette man fell to the ground, rolling to his side and reaching for a knife in his pocket. James kicked him hard in the ribs, once, twice, three times, then toed the man onto his back.

He bent down, and gingerly picked up the man's cigarette from the ground. James took a long drag, exhaled slowly, then flicked the cigarette into the man's open mouth. The girl had stopped screaming and stood there crying quietly.

James brushed the blood and dirt from his hands and felt for the matches in his pocket. He pulled them out and tossed them. With his foot, James turned the man on his side. The man groaned in pain.

"Shut up," James said. He reached his hand into the man's pocket and pulled out the lighter. He flicked it to check that it worked, then stood up and walked away.

Halfway to the street, he looked back and saw her helping him to his feet, her long dark hair falling like a shield around him. The man batted her arms away and steadied himself against the wall. She used the hem of her dress to wipe dirt from his pants, the thin muscles of her back showing where the dress dipped low. James considered this, considered her, and turned and kept walking down the alley. He regretted coming to this bar, regretted this whole trip. He turned toward his hotel and the pool and an air-conditioned casino with umbrellas in the drinks.

GHOST WALK

Greta Boris

Cecily and I waited for almost an hour to be scared. Laser lights flickered in the dark treetops like disembodied souls. They no longer chilled me. Not even the theme song from *The Exorcist* that floated through the outdoor speakers raised goosebumps on my arms.

Cecily rested her head on my chest, and emitted the sound a teakettle makes before it boils. "Mommy, how much longer?"

"We're in the next group. Just a couple more minutes."

"You said that forever ago."

I patted her silky head but didn't answer. I *had* said that forever ago. In San Juan Capistrano, Halloween is celebrated each year with a Ghost Walk. The neighborhood it's set in is touted as the oldest and most haunted residential community in California. I thought it was a perfect spot for a scare-fest, and based on the numbers in the queue, most of Southern Orange County agreed with me.

"Next group," squeaked a Historical Society volunteer as the mob pressed toward her. Cecily threaded her skinny arm through mine and pulled me forward with surprising strength. Nothing stands in the way of a determined nine-year-old.

"Good evening." Our docent, a pale woman in black, did

a pretty fair imitation of Alfred Hitchcock. "Thank you for joining us."

Our group gathered around her. "Tonight, we'll visit some of the earliest inhabitants of San Juan Capistrano. They are an emotional lot, easily upset, and when disturbed they tend to be unpredictable. I strongly suggest you remain close and keep your voices down."

"Hands and arms in at all times," my daughter said under her breath, mimicking the ride operators at Disneyland. She'd inherited her father's dry wit. My jaw tightened. This was the third time since we'd arrived that Rob had injected his unwanted presence into my thoughts.

The first time was when I'd noticed the ticket seller's hair curling over his forehead like Rob's had. Then I'd heard the laugh. Someone in the crowd had erupted with Rob's deep belly laugh.

"Mom, come on," Cecily yanked my arm. Our tour guide glided out of the light and up Los Rios Street. We followed en masse with a swish of fabric and a slap of shoes. In a half-block a howl stopped us cold.

Although I knew it was an act, the hair on my arms stood at attention. Cecily, who'd skipped ahead of me, did an about-face. She plastered herself to my back and peeked out from under my arm.

"Where are they?" a voice wailed. "My children. Where are my children?" A corpse-faced specter in a tattered charcoal dress seemed to fly at our circle.

I knew this legend. It was the tale of La Llorona, a young woman seduced by a soldier who made promises he never kept. Many cultures had versions of it.

I could relate to men not keeping promises, but not to La Llorona's solution to the problem. Cecily circled me and moved to the front of the crowd. I resisted the urge to pull her away.

The story had a gruesome end.

La Llorona dropped into a stage whisper, and the group quieted to catch the words. "I did something I regret to this day. I took my children down to the creek when the water was high. One by one, I threw them into its foamy depths."

A snort sounded close to my left ear. A lovely, dark-eyed woman with skin almost as brown as mine stood next to me. "Stupid cow." Her vehemence surprised me. "I don't have patience with victims."

I didn't know what to say, so I didn't say anything. I agreed with her on general principle, but this was a ghost walk, a play. It wasn't worth being militant about.

I watched Cecily's face, wondering how she would react to the tragic story. She stood at the edge of the circle, staring at the moaning La Llorona. As I walked toward her, a wisp of smoke wrapped around her head, and I smelled tobacco. This was a family friendly event. I turned to look for the smoking culprit, prepared to give him or her a piece of my mind.

A man in a gray sweater locked gazes with me. He pulled a cigar the size of a Rottweiler's scat from his shirt pocket, but it was unlit. "Mind if I smoke?" He grinned with teeth so yellow I assumed this wasn't a new habit.

"I'd rather you didn't," I said in a cool voice. He shrugged and stuck the tip of the stogie between his lips and chewed.

I scanned the other faces around me but couldn't find the source of the smoke. What I did see, however, surprised me. Our small group had almost doubled in size, and the new members all wore period costumes. The females had on skirts that fell to mid-calf and the males wore cotton trousers and button-up shirts instead of jeans and T-shirts. Apparently, people got into the spirit of this thing.

Our docent waved a hand and beckoned us on. Cecily slid next to me, grabbed my hand, and pulled ahead. We separated a young Hispanic couple and wove through a harried woman's passel of raven-haired children.

"Modesta Avila, how are you this fine night?" our docent said to an actor dressed in clothes from the turn of the nineteenth century. We'd left La Llorona behind and moved up Los Rios to a ramshackle wooden building, gray with age. A woman stood on its front porch under a sign that read, The Hummingbird House Cafe.

"I'm mad as a wet hen," Modesta spit the words. This actor, a young, attractive woman with caramel skin, was a very different ghost from La Llorona.

"Why is that, Modesta? What's happened?"

The ghost went on to tell the tale of Orange County's first convicted felon, Modesta Avila. The woman she portrayed was sent to the state penitentiary for obstructing the train tracks to protest the railroad company's seizure of her land.

"She has backbone." The dark-eyed woman was at my side again.

The docent either didn't hear her or chose to ignore her. She waved a white hand toward Modesta and said, "I heard they sent you to San Quentin."

"They did. I was the first female inmate." A proud expression crossed Modesta's face. "But I wasn't there for hanging laundry across the tracks. Don't believe what you've heard. Those were excuses. They arrested me because I was going to have a little one, and I wasn't married." Modesta pivoted to the side and smoothed her skirt over her abdomen to show the audience her bump.

The dark-eyed woman next to me tensed. "The power of prejudice, that's what it was." I wasn't sure if this was addressed to me or all of San Juan Capistrano, so I didn't respond.

Besides, the topic made me uncomfortable. Rob and I had never married. When I found out I was pregnant, we were still in college. He wanted to finish up, get a job with a decent paycheck and have a nice wedding. The white dress would look better if I weren't sporting a baby-in-the-making. That's what he'd said, anyway.

At the time I'd thought, why not? Who cared about bourgeois niceties, the obsolete restrictions of our parents' generation? What a mistake that turned out to be.

"I spent almost three years in prison, but just before my release date, I died." Modesta uttered her last line.

The dark-eyed beauty in the audience turned to leave, and I noticed she was pregnant too. My hand fluttered to my empty abdomen. I had once wanted more children and was sure Rob felt the same. During my pregnancy he'd been loving and thoughtful. He accommodated my cravings and was patient with my mood swings. If someone had told me he'd abandon us, I wouldn't have believed them.

The audience hummed and shifted, anxious to move on. Where was Cecily? I stood on tiptoes and peered over the crowd. "Cecily," I called.

"Mommy, ready?" She appeared from behind me. The streetlamps glinted off her curly brown hair and flickered in the midnight blue of her eyes—eyes like her father's. She smiled. The bow of her mouth became Rob's.

A memory stabbed me with such ferocity, the hand resting on my stomach clenched. I was on the street in San Clemente. Rob had taken me to see a three-piece jazz ensemble. It was our first date, and I'd had one-too-many glasses of wine to settle my nerves. When we stepped out into the salty evening air, I reached for him. The moment my lips met his, I fell hopelessly in love.

He'd told me he felt the same. The hole his betrayal tore in my heart wouldn't mend, despite my efforts to forget him. I'd lost him before his death, I just hadn't known it then.

"Ahem." The man in the gray sweater broke into my thoughts. He sat on the porch rail of the Hummingbird, his head above the crowd. When the hum of voices quieted, he took his unlit cheroot from his mouth and cleared his throat. "Please continue in an orderly fashion to the next entertainment station."

Period costumes swept the ground as we followed his instructions. Cecily and I must have switched groups in the shuffle. The sweater man was our new docent.

We came to a dark, vacant lot on Los Rios Street. The ruins of the mission's Great Stone Church stood out behind it in dramatic relief. A hooded figure dressed in a monk's robe waited for us. His face was hidden under the shadow of the cowl. A tingle of fear traveled over my skin.

Only a handful of children remained with the adults in our group, which included my pregnant friend, the young Hispanic lovers Cecily had plowed between earlier, and our cigar-gnawing leader. Would this ghost be too scary for Cecily? Was that why the others had left early? I gripped her hand.

When the rustling ceased, the hooded figure pointed to the ruins. A nasal voice, completely unlike the Darth Vader tones I expected, came from beneath the cowl. "On December 8, 1812, forty worshipers entered the Great Stone Church to celebrate mass. Among them was a beautiful young girl called Magdalena."

Cecily squirmed at my side. "What's wrong?" I said.

"What's that?" She said.

"What's what?"

"In the window." Cecily pointed at a window high up in the ruins.

I saw a flame flicker there, then go out. A nervous moth batted its wings in my stomach. There was nothing behind that church wall—no building, no room, no floor, nothing. A candle would have to hover in thin air to appear there. "I didn't see anything," I lied.

"Teofilo sat in the congregation," the monk continued his narrative. "His face shone like the sun when he looked on his lovely Magdalena. But instead of filling her with joy, it consumed her with grief. They could never be together. Her father wouldn't allow it."

What was it with fathers? Rob's father was the villain of my story as well. It was his interference that ruined our relationship.

Rob went to see his father when Cecily was three. We'd decided we'd waited long enough. We were going to marry with or without his blessing, but Rob wanted to give him one last chance to do the right thing.

Four days later, instead of coming home Rob sent a strangely worded email. He used expressions I'd never heard him use, said things I couldn't imagine coming from his mouth. In the last line, he wrote that he needed time to *carefully consider* our future together. Carefully consider? We'd been discussing it for years. I couldn't imagine what his father had said to create such doubt, but I was sure Rob would come to his senses. I still believed he loved me.

Cecily shifted next to me. This evening was a bad idea. Ghosts from my past had risen along with San Juan Capistrano's. The monk's voice grated. The schmaltzy Romeo and Juliet story annoyed me. I kept catching whiffs of something that smelled like burning dog turds, but whenever my eyes met the man's in the gray sweater, his cigar was unlit.

"Let's go," I said to Cecily.

"No, please." She looked at me with alarm. "I want to hear what happened."

I stayed, but this was the last ghost. Then I'd go home, have a glass of wine, and mourn in peace.

Mourn in peace? Where had that thought come from? I wasn't mourning. I'd stopped all that two years, three months, five days, and fourteen hours after I got the call that Rob's body had been found in the woods near his family's hunting cabin. I remembered the moment exactly.

Rob's father had finally died. I say finally, because the selfish old coot hung on long after lung cancer would have taken out most men. I went to the reading of the will when I received the invitation. Not because I expected anything for myself. I knew how Rob's father felt about me, but I thought he might have left something to his only grandchild—to Cecily.

Every surviving relative from elderly aunts to obscure second cousins were called out by name and left an amount of money or some other thing of value. His business partners and employees were called up next. Each received at least a token. The final endowment was a solitaire diamond set in a platinum band. That was given to his housekeeper.

The lawyer closed the folder of paperwork, glanced up and gave me an apologetic smile. I felt my cheeks burn, whether with anger or embarrassment it was hard to say. Probably both. As the group dispersed, I crossed to where the lawyer sat gathering his things.

"Why did you invite me if there was nothing in the will for my daughter?" My words came in a breathless rush. I had to get them out while I could still talk. Tears threatened to shut down my vocal cords.

"It was a provision of the will," he said.

"What do you mean?"

"He said he'd carefully considered it and wanted you to hear the will read."

Carefully considered. The cruelty of those words, the same words Rob had used in his email, echoed through me all the way home from L.A. I'd known Rob's father didn't like me. I was the poor hussy from the other side of the tracks who'd tried to trap his son through pregnancy. But I'd believed in Rob's love.

On that drive, I accepted the truth. Rob and I wouldn't have married even if he hadn't died cleaning his gun. I'd tried to convince myself he would have come home, but how could that be true? If he'd cared about me, about Cecily, he wouldn't have had anything to consider. He wouldn't have accepted his father's views, parroted his exact words. Rob's father was toxic. He'd poisoned his son.

At the junction of the 405 and 5 freeways, I made a decision. I was done mourning Rob. He'd chosen his father and his inheritance over me and Cecily. I chose to relegate his memory to my closet of past mistakes and slam the door.

"Suddenly," the pitch of the monk's voice startled me to attention. "The earth shook. The worshipers jumped to their feet and ran for the doors, but it was too late. The building collapsed. They were buried under the walls of stone.

"When the rubble was cleared away, the body of a young girl was discovered still holding a candle in one hand and a young man's hand with the other. Magdalena and Teofilo were together at last. It's said Magdalena's candle can still be seen in the window of the Great Stone Church on half-moon nights."

Cecily sighed. "That's so romantic. Don't you think?"

I didn't have the heart to say no, so I nodded. "Time to go."

Several moments passed before I realized Cecily and I were alone on Los Rios Street. Not even the man in the gray sweater walked with us. I turned to see if we'd left them all behind, but the street was empty.

A black, flickering shadow the size of a small bus slid across the landscape toward the Great Stone Church ruins. The silhouettes of two individuals holding hands trailed behind it, making me think of Magdalena and Teofilo.

I stared at the strange sight until I was startled by a sheet of white paper fluttering past. The wind cemented it to the side of a trash can long enough for me to read the words printed on it in a large Old Western font—*Ghost Walk.* Then it blew away.

Ghosts walk? Do they? My gaze darted to the vacant lot. The dark cloud I'd seen had reached the church ruins now. As I watched, it thinned and disappeared into the stones. The shadow couple followed. They touched the wall and were gone, as if they'd been absorbed. A cold sweat slicked my forehead.

Cecily dragged along next to me, chatting about Maggie and Teo like they were old friends, not appearing to notice our isolation. "Did you—" I stopped. I wasn't sure what I'd just seen and didn't want to fill my daughter with strange ideas. "Hurry," I said instead. "I'm cold."

Cecily dropped my hand and skipped ahead. "Don't go too far." My voice crackled with worry.

"You said to hurry." Her words floated in a singsong over her shoulder.

I wrapped my arms around myself and picked up my pace. I could see the O'Neill Museum, where we'd waited in line, in the distance. The museum was located in the Old Pryor house. Legend had it that Albert Pryor, who'd died of a stroke in his fifties, still visited its front porch to rock in a ghostly rocking chair. That didn't seem so far-fetched tonight.

The building was quiet now. No laser lights danced in the trees. No music floated down the street. No cars were parked out front. Mine was in the lot on the other side of the train tracks. I longed to be safely behind the wheel with Cecily seat-belted in the back, and the doors locked. The eerie emptiness of the night and the questions it raised scared me more than any performance could.

I jumped at the whistle of an approaching train. The sound was followed quickly by the clanging of alarms. Cecily, hearing the noise, broke into a run and headed straight for the crossing.

"No, Cecily! Wait for me." I yelled, but my voice was swallowed by the din. I ran toward the crossing and got there just in time to see my daughter scoot under the red and white gate as it dropped into position. By the time she reached the platform on the other side, the train was upon us.

Panic flooded through me. As soon as the train passed, I would cross the tracks, take Cecily's hand, and we'd walk together to the parking garage. She would be fine. I told myself all this, but the feeling of terror that had come over me when I saw her brown head duck beneath the barrier wouldn't leave.

I searched for her between the rushing train cars. Nothing. Then I saw a blue jean clad leg and red tennis shoe.

Then a train car passed. I saw all of her. Then a train car. The images ran together in the stilted manner of an old animated movie. She left the frame. Returned with a man.

A man. A band of fear wrapped around my chest as another train car flew by.

She and the man hugged. Train car.

They stepped apart. Train car.

He held her by both hands.

I could only see the man's profile and that only in brief intervals, but there was something familiar about the way he stood. The curl of hair falling on his forehead. I choked back a sob.

When the last car thundered past, I saw my daughter only yards away. Her face glowed. I darted across the tracks and hugged her hard. She allowed it for a moment then pushed me away.

"Who was that?" I said.

"Daddy." She held out her hand. Something glinted in her palm. "He said to give you this."

I swallowed the fear rising in my throat and reached for the object. It was cool to my touch, small and bright. I lifted it from her hand and held it up.

A ring. A beautiful solitaire diamond set in platinum. It looked like the one Rob and I had admired in a jewelry store window two months before he'd died. It looked like the one his father's housekeeper had inherited. My finger touched a rough place on the inside of the band.

I stepped closer to a streetlamp. Something was etched there. I rotated the ring until the light fell on the writing. There was only one word—*forever.*

* * *

I don't remember getting to the car. Memories I'd stopped up long ago broke their dam. My heart and mind were flooded. Image after image, scene after scene, cascaded over me. Rob giving me my first and only surfing lesson. Wine tasting in Paso Robles. A Jacuzzi on a small porch overlooking the ocean. The delight on his face when I told him I was pregnant. Cecily as an infant, snuggled against his bare chest.

I sat behind the wheel of the car and stared through the windshield at the cement wall in front of me. Grief and joy mingled into an emotion I couldn't name. Cecily dozed next to me, her small hand resting on my leg.

I didn't believe in ghosts. They were the stuff of legends and movies. But tonight, my carefully constructed world view had crumbled like the Great Stone Church in the 1812 earthquake.

I put a hand on Cecily's shoulder and gave her a gentle shake. "I didn't think you remembered your dad."

"I do," Cecily said, without opening her eyes. "Kind of." Her calm acceptance of the evening's events made no sense, but then nothing made sense about this night.

"How can you be sure it was him? He died a long time ago. You were only three."

Instead of answering my question, she touched the ring on my finger. "Did he give you that?"

Her memory of his appearance seemed to be dissolving as rapidly as the ring. I could now see my skin through the band which had become as transparent as glass. I took a few jagged breaths. "We should go."

Cecily gave me a tired smile and climbed over the seat into the back. She was sound asleep before we exited the parking structure.

The car bumped across the railroad tracks, and a thought jostled into my mind. I'd been given a gift. Not the ring. I glanced at the sparkling stone. All that was left of it was a two-karat orb of light that would be gone before I reached home. No, I'd been given a gift of knowledge.

Rob had purchased the ring. He'd already decided to marry me before that trip to his father's house. He wouldn't have given it to his father, yet it ended up in the old man's possession. I'd seen it at the reading of the will.

The ring fitted into the puzzle of Rob's death and changed the entire picture. I'd always been bothered by the chronology of events, but the avalanche of emotions I'd felt at the time had destroyed logic.

Rob had left home on a Friday. He was found the following Thursday. The medical examiner's report had said he'd been dead four to five days. His email had come on Monday. At the time, one day had seemed insignificant, a mistake. No longer.

The strangely worded email that had sounded so much like his father, must have been his father. Whether the old man had shot his only child in a fit of rage, or whether it had truly been an accident, I would never know. But I did know Rob hadn't abandoned me. The dead communicated, the incidents of the evening proved that, but they didn't do it by email.

I made a left onto Los Rios Street and drove toward the O'Neill Museum. Tonight, a wrong was divinely righted. Justice reached into the grave and brought me out the truth. Rob and I may never have married, but the old man hadn't won. Rob loved me. He'd bought the ring, and there was a forever. The knowledge I'd gained wouldn't stand up in a court of law, but it was enough for me.

As I neared the O'Neill Museum, a flame flickered to life, blue against black. When it went out, I could see the man in the gray sweater sitting on the porch in the light of the half-moon. He waved at me from his rocking chair as I drove past.

I shot a glance into the rearview mirror, doubting my eyes. A warm red glow filled my field of vision, followed by a cloud of smoke. He'd finally lit that damn cigar.

THE EDGE

S.J. Haworth

They get on my case in group. Some of the others freak on the hot seat. Me, I stay composed and stick to short replies; but it's tricky keeping secrets from this ragtag gang of loonies. They can spot a liar as fast as I can.

I never speak Julian's name here.

Stalling for time, I turn my face to the open window and breathe in delicate afternoon fragrance. Jasmine, I think.

Strident voices snap me back. Admit it, they demand, you're in danger.

The thought maybe they're right worms into my head, but I douse the ping of icy awareness and try to ignore its mustard seed of self-preservation.

Vague but cooperative, I say, "I fell down the stairs." Of course, they don't believe me. I make allowances for projection. Several of them come from abuse.

A few got here by mandate from judges; some straggled in from a post-psych ward. I don't belong here. It's not like I need therapy. I joined up to pacify my late husband George. My outbursts bothered him. After he got killed, I continued for other reasons.

There are steps you can take, they insist.

Such a fuss over a cracked radius. I'm not clear how it happened myself. Julian was there, but pills don't mix well with alcohol, so who can tell? I don't mention the couple of drinks to anyone. I get tired of being scolded. I *am* twenty-six.

George tried to curb my excesses. He was big on self-restraint. Everyone has an agenda.

Maybe the lost don't, which would make them innocent. The rest of us latch onto someone else's hunger. George captured me to make his life interesting, then complained when I did. Things got a little out of hand after that.

"Fell down the stairs," therapist Barbie, our group facilitator, repeats with a noddy, nod, nod, nod, like a bobble-head dog trinket in a car's rear window. I almost laugh. She adds, "Hmmm. That's a bit cliché, don't you think?" Barbie is fifty, same age as poor deceased George. She wears a polka-dot bow perched on top of her 1950s, big-curl bangs that bounce bravely somewhere between Betty and Veronica.

I think you should check your head in a mirror—talk about clichés. *Barbie.*

My face expressionless, I slink her a sideways glance. I think I'd better take care. Her cheery Alice-after-Wonderland act doesn't fool me. It camouflages an insatiable curiosity for hidden skeletons, and a hound dog's nose for ferreting them out.

Fat Annie, teacher's pet, says, "Face it, honey. This guy's bad news. You gotta get rid of him before it's too late."

For a fraction I teeter on the brink of her point of view. Then I come to my senses. Brave strong words, but she isn't the one who has to walk into the lung-emptying void. Alone.

"Believe me, we all understand how hard it is." Only thing this tight-assed old virgin knows is how to keep the focus off her own broken self.

"Denial." Mousey Mary nods like a pro.

I grit my teeth and give Mousey my evil look from under my brows to frighten her back into her hole.

Long Tall Lily, our oldest member, puts a supportive arm

around Mousey. No one comforts me. I rub damp palms on my chair arms and look out at a tree. Sphinx-like, my persona calm, I stifle inappropriate urges to cross socially accepted lines.

Amusing how their frustration with me mounts when I don't argue. A deep breath of satisfaction helps remind me my style is more seducer; I get my way with whispers. Recently, upon request, I added obedient to my repertoire. Unable to stop it, my private smile comes out.

"This isn't a joke, Griselda." Fat Annie again, serious and stern this time. Prissy bitch proves even the deeply depressed can claim their power if they try.

My eyes water up. I tell them, "Lay off, okay?" Chin on chest, I hang my head over my ace bandage. I left the sling at home. It seemed too dramatic.

Surrender doesn't stop this ill-assorted gaggle of personality disorders.

"We're trying to help you." Lily uses that singsong sugariness they call passive-aggressive. She's good at it. I'm better.

Yeah, I get my money's worth, one way or another. Therapy helps clear my thoughts and sharpen my people skills. Difficult situations like, well, Julian, need handling.

He'd be furious if he knew I was here. He thinks I quit coming. Says it's dangerous. My mouth might overstep the safety zone. Is he looking out for me or himself? I spend a minute on doubt. He should know by now I'm loyal.

"You're evading." Mousey tries her hand at confrontation. "Offense is a weak defense."

"Oh, yeah? Tell that to Lao Tsu," I snap.

"We worry about you out there by yourself." Therapist Barbie takes control gently. "You live in a pretty isolated area."

My head comes up fast. "Are you talking to me?" Her switching topics momentarily confuses me. They do things like that in therapy. I don't even snigger at my *Taxi Driver* movie reference. "How do you know that? Did you do a drive-by? Are you spying on me?" I wouldn't put it past her.

"No, of course not. You told us about your property."

I did?

My mind instantly goes to the angular glassy structure that George—may he rest in peace—built around me in the sage-scented foothills southwest of Palomar Mountain.

Julian Trask, our landscape architect, helped me break free. I didn't understand his part in it two years ago, when we started. Some epiphanies come more slowly than others.

I lick my lips and taste sex from earlier. Musky male scent lingers on me. I inhale Julian on my breath and on my red-tipped fingers. Now I'm the smug one.

Smiling to myself I clear my throat and say, "The property is isolated, but I'm not lonely." Even when the desert emptiness sucks at the in-between places. "I like my privacy." I inherited the house after the police finally backed off.

I haven't let myself love owning the place yet, just in case. I'm good at resisting.

Someone asks me a question, but I get distracted picturing police hunched over their magnifying glasses, examining aspects of my life. Forensic hotshots found drugs in George's system, same type as my prescriptions. Suspicious, the cops called it. Insurance investigators agreed and dug their toes in over settling up. City Hall held up probate. They just recently released the body for burial. Julian suggested cremation. I hope George didn't mind.

Like she read my mind, Barbie says, "It's a lot to deal with, being widowed, then a police investigation. Maybe it's time we—"

Before I can stop myself, I bang my good fist on a nearby side table. Kitschy trinkets and a box of Kleenex judder. "No!" I shout. "That's *off limits.*" I sneak a peek at the shocked faces. "Sorry." The girls look so fragile, I dial back the agitation and say in a moderate tone, "I don't want to talk about it." My lips fold tightly together.

No way am I going to let them rake up stuff about detectives taking me in for questioning. Over and over I told Sergeant This and Lieutenant That that George had access to my drugs; I couldn't control him. In return, they made me admit I was half his age. I asked if they'd discovered that by calculator. When they weren't badgering me, we had some fun conversations. Really, I felt quite flattered they thought I could organize a car crash. No one mentioned Julian.

Which gets me thinking, I haven't seen any cops since they released George's remains. Weird, I miss them. Another loss. I almost mention this emotion to the group, but don't. It might lead into dangerous territory. So I stick to the rules and keep my trap shut.

I hear rustling. Barbie plumps a cushion. We're alone. Mysteriously, while I was mulling things over, the others left.

"It's Friday," she says. Translation, she and her husband are booked to do something couples-y.

"Oh," I'm suddenly reluctant to leave her newly built room above the garage, added for clients, top-heavy and lop-sided, but deductible. I complimented the finishes once for something to say. "Okay." I rise to leave kind of wishing I could stay and unload the whole truth to her.

Once, to prolong things, I repeated Julian's opinion there is no unconscious. Collective or otherwise, he says it's a crock. Barbie pretty much lost it, the way people do when you cast doubt on their religion. How was I to know she'd get hot under the collar about the myths of her vocation? We all guard our uncertainties.

So I don't open up to the therapist. Maybe I should quit.

"See you next week." She's tidying up, moving it along.

"Yeah, sure," I say over my shoulder as I descend the stairs.

Isolation clamps around my chest like the flu. The sick feeling grows with each step. The flat of my hand drags along the plaster. My feet slow. I remember I have to meet Julian at his Mensa party. Mine too, now.

The thought triggers that vile blue, nihilistic color. My lover had I certified officially smart. Another hurdle for me to leap. He keeps raising the bar. In this instance, the test was multiple choice and made me an eligible *parti* to membership in his club where words get leveled like missiles.

"You tested high," he'd said, eyes narrowed on me, assessing. No congratulation. I thought he would be pleased. Now he's considering moving on to a more exclusive gang of smarties, Prometheus. Clever way to abandon me. That hurts.

Does he purposely pull these about-faces to unhinge me?

Off-handedly, he'd added, "Bring your jewelry if you want." I design jewelry to sell and carry samples in the car. I have contracts with Neiman and Bloomies. My wares can stay in the trunk. The brainiacs don't buy enough for me to bother, and I don't need their validation. But I do tuck my special stash into the tiny sequined shoulder-strap purse.

Julian's van isn't outside the Poway ranch house when I arrive half an hour later. I park across the street. A reprieve? I dread crowds, they scramble my synapses.

He's probably moving equipment to the band's next gig. Lead guitarist, his new calling. He's good, too, maybe on the brink of making it big with his hot electric eyes and macho menace strutting around the stage, steaming up the audience in that heavy metal kind of way. I'm already bracing for groupies.

People start arriving. I hang back and wait near the car. A few acknowledge my existence with cool hellos. I go in anyway. Julian will expect it. I don't want to be here, but I jump through every hoop. Rebellion rises like acid at the back of my throat.

Inside, geniuses catapult over one another's verbs. A woman thrusts a tall aqua drink with an umbrella into my hand and says she's my hostess. "This your first meeting, dear?" I tell her, no, it isn't. She says, really? Why would I lie? Dubious, she considers my designer getup, incongruous at a gathering full of gingham-wrapped dowds. When she turns away, I set the glass down. You never know. It could be fatal.

In moments, another woman offers me a lumpy, homemade cookie. "Here, taste this." She insists I eat it. "It's a new recipe." She hovers.

My stomach clenches.

I swallowed Julian this morning. A salty sea of sperm. Always a challenge, but I came up to scratch. Am I Golden Bough stronger now? A rare feeling of self-assurance steals over me.

The cookie sticks in my throat.

The room fills up with claustrophobia. Scathing, scalding syllables splice between bombs of unconnected, but well-informed paragraphs. Intellect talks a lot. I'd like to leave but stay and watch fine minds get pickled. In one of those visual shifts that comes with increasing frequency, I watch them aim elephant trunkfuls of Bristol Cream sherry at each other.

Maybe it's my new scripts. I wasn't tranquil enough on Xanax and trazodone, so Dr. Deeds added clonazepam. The DSM says that's an anti-psychotic. I always check. You can't trust doctors. So far, I feel nothing.

Julian told me to stop taking all that shit. Says it's like volunteering to go flatline ahead of schedule. He wants me to feel everything.

Movement catches my attention. A glass oblong container, one-third full of a peculiar blue liquid sits on a rickety melamine shelf. The foul cerulean fluid sways up and down, up and down, oozing slowly from side to side. I shudder. I can't tear my eyes away. It's hypnotic, hideous, terrible. The color of nausea. Sartre would understand.

I dust powdered sugar from the cookie off my fingers and edge carefully around clumps of people but get pinned against a table full of bottles and a punch bowl. I plan to stay away from alcohol tonight; you never know where it's going to lead.

More people arrive. My therapist, Barbie, walks in. Now that's what I call shock treatment. Is she following me? She's with a big, red-faced man who's glad-handing his way into the room. Interesting. The husband I presume. *Oh my.* I know him. He and Julian are friends. We hung out with him a few times. I last saw Ben at a Summer Solstice ceremony. Witchy stuff in a clearing. Pretty lame. Julian went off somewhere without me. I got annoyed and let this guy feel me up. Well, well, Big Ben. Small world. North County communities are like villages.

Barbie and I avoid each other's eyes.

"Get the Trivial Pursuits, Ben's here," someone calls out.

Instantly I see a herd of Mensans leaping like goats from square to square on a gigantic game board. Someone bumps into me. My vision clears. It's a sign. On the spot, I decide to stop swallowing pills. First, I need to make sure my nerves are under control. I mustn't unravel again.

My moody lover thinks it's time we live together. I always prefer the status quo, whatever it is. He's instructed me to sell the glass monstrosity so we can buy an estate together in posh Rancho Santa Fe with my double indemnity payoff. Julian has a rattling big house in his sights; a haunted hallways kind of thing. Type of place where you expect to come across a dungeon with chains. Ten acres of land. Privacy to scream, he told me with a laugh.

All of a sudden, I don't want that to happen. An epiphany. I *face* it. I *own* that bit of truth. I admit to myself I want out.

Queasy with fear I teeter on the brink of a dicey decision while I stand squashed in by Julian's Mensans. My trembling fingers unzip the sequin purse hanging by my hip. A zing of panic ripples down my spine. I look lovingly at a bottle of Scotch.

Finally, my therapist and I acknowledge each other's existence. Tight smile. She doesn't want me here. We both try to move on, but we're temporarily hemmed in together by the crowd. Barbie, reluctant but trapped, speaks to me.

"So, are you Mensa?"

I admit it.

She looks around possessively and says, "They're good

people." She's the type who only knows good people in any situation. Bad people are more interesting. "You never mentioned it." An accusation.

Should I say, neither did you? What's the etiquette here? "It's recent."

We chat, stiff as two cockerels. She does introductions. Turns out, Ben's a therapist too, a circuit speaker not a one-on-one or group facilitator. Julian rarely bothers with conventional details and, of course, I never mention Barbie to him.

Laughing, Big Ben greets me with a booming hello, then a blank stare. He's drunk already, has no memory of meeting me. He does this every time we meet. I used to think it was a put-down. Tonight, I assume he doesn't want Barbie to know what he gets up to.

I tuck this morsel away for later inspection. Given the right provocation, I might tell Barbie how Druid get-togethers act as an aphrodisiac on her spouse. Bet that would throw her. I could mention denial, for fun.

Husbands shouldn't get off too easily. I say, "We've met."

Ben snaps his fingers as though with sudden memory. "You sell beads!" I give him a blank face. He takes another boozy stab at it. "You're Julian's girlfriend."

Uh-oh. Too late, I realize my mistake.

Barbie turns her head and studies me, putting it together. My heart thumps horribly.

Ben looks from me to his wife. "Shit! You're a client, aren't you? Oops. Awwwkward." He grins like a naughty boy and throws his wife a glittering challenging look.

I feel myself go white as my safety net unravels.

Julian will go lethal if he hears I lied to him about leaving therapy. My mind scrabbles frantically to remember everything I've said over the past two years. Impossible.

Gawping and defenseless, I stretch my lips wide into a chimpanzee smile of my own. I busy my hands ladling aqua liquid from the punch bowl into a glass.

Barbie takes away the bottle of beer Ben just picked up and says to everyone within earshot, "You've had enough. Remember, we're driving Francis and Lou home."

Almost as an afterthought I stir an unhealthy dollop of special powder into the blue brew that is my drink with an umbrella stem. I top it off with mint leaves and a Maraschino cherry.

Ben's twitch of annoyance whips Barbie's way. "Don't nag me, wife." He shoves his way roughly through the crowd, smacking a redhead on the bottom as he passes. In the center of the room he stops and raises both arms above his head, calling out, "May I have your attention, ladies, gents, and others." He takes charge like a Vegas impresario. Surprisingly, he's a pretty good stand-up comic. After a few minutes' patter he pauses, grinning. "I'll be happy to moderate your trivial pursuits." That gets a laugh. "And the winner gets Barbie." More laughter.

A heckler calls out, "You're in trouble now, Benjy."

Wife Barbie, shoulders straight, posture good-sport perky, aims a tense smile randomly at the universe. I saw her having coffee with George once, looking like that. I assumed they were talking about me. Now I wonder. I tap a fingernail against the glass.

Julian comes in through the open patio slider. He moves along the wall behind Ben. Julian prefers the edges of a room. He ignores me.

I laugh in a trilling way and sense Barbie looking at me, but I can't take my eyes off Julian. Ruthless, focused, intense. Sporadically gregarious. He draws a crowd of his own in a stand-back-askance-sardonic-expression kind of way. Do people like him? Do I? He has a dark aura. My flavor.

"I'm not afraid of him," I say out loud by accident.

Barbie's eyes are on me instantly. I glimpse speculation vying with something else I can't name, but it worries me.

I can't help myself, my gaze returns to Julian, fixes on him, craving his attention. I need him to focus on me the way he did in the beginning. Back when he took me ballroom dancing in a tatty, older strip mall. The music had vibrated through the shabby dance floor and rapturous rhythm had strummed on my pulse. He introduced me to rhumba and the Argentine tango, among other things.

Julian catches me watching him. The faint smile in his eyes taunts my neediness with sly knowing. Odd how his mockery tantalizes me. He knows I want to touch him, but he's being circumspect. I drag my gaze away.

Ben finishes his spiel, hands the pack of questions over to someone and goes outside on the patio with a flask he produces, and Julian. My gaze follows them as they disappear from view.

A wave of exhaustion laps round my knees. Someone has stolen my chi. It takes effort to remain upright.

Barbie has the thousand-yard stare of a woman wondering where her husband goes at night without her. She's wide open, her soft place unprotected. Eyes on the patio, Barbie says she hasn't seen Julian Trask in a long time. She's waiting for me to tell her he's the one who broke my arm. I don't think she's made all the connections yet. It comes to me they're enemies, Julian and Barbie. I can use that.

I lift the aqua drink to my mouth. Barbie takes it from me. I knew she would. "It's yours." I sigh as though resigned, and glance toward the patio. Her eyes follow mine, so suggestible. Her face hardens with a spasm of defiance. Good. I read her right.

At last, the bottle neck clears. We smile tepid goodbyes, but before I can move on, Barbie places a hand on my wrist as though she wants to say something. She's wearing the ring I made her, perfect on her white skin. I pause to admire my design. It's exquisite.

While she hesitates, I almost have second thoughts, but walk away half listening to snippets of conversations. Out of the corner of my eye I see her gazing into the glass she took from me. It's up to the universe now. I head for a bar on the other side of the room, this time for whisky and ginger beer. I add ice, juice of a lemon, plenty of sugar and mint. A full-bodied tipple Julian likes. I tap in additive and stir briskly.

Nearby a man in a tired tweed jacket with elbow patches says, "Happiness, yeah. Like that's what life is all about." I admire his jawline, his shoulders, his shaggy yellow hair. I'm glad I painted my nails Fire Engine Red. They belong in public view. Blondie notices me and comes over. My Versace perfume gives me confidence and tells the world I'm ready for use. He natters on for a while, saying things like, "It behooves us to take responsibility. So I went like totally green last year." I nod like Barbie. Participating.

He steps it up with, "I mean, let's face it. Human nature is what it is, right?" A wave of boredom almost kills the deal, but he's so beautiful I accept his vapid mantras and smile back at him. He's enjoying me, too, in an empty, party flirtation kind of way. When he asks me about myself, I get excited and jabber on too long.

I revive like a wilted plant and lean toward him. My tongue runs across my lips. I enjoy being the center of his sensual, half-lidded attention. A small ache of human longing nibbles at me, the ordinary kind. I'm ready for something—less taxing. We get twenty, low-watt, silly verbal minutes together exchanging inanities.

Julian returns.

Sparking awareness slaps me awake. My lips part on a deep inhale, like an infant's first welcome-to-earth gasp. He grips my waist hard from behind. I feel outdoor cold on his jacket. His hot breath hits the nape of my neck. Tantric male energy blows me into a raw, voluptuous, cobweb-shattering state of readiness.

I struggle against this gale force. I've made up my mind. It's not safe. But I quiver under the assault and forget the world. Heat pools between my legs, the core of me aflame. Rubbery, comatose flesh comes alive with pins and needles.

Exultant, I exist again.

I turn around in his arms to face him. The glass of bourbon rests between us. He looks down and puts his hands over mine, raising the glass to my mouth. I dip my tongue into golden liquid, then lick the rim with a sultry invitational look. We both ignore the commotion when a woman collapses.

The corners of my mouth tilt up. Looks like I'm done with therapy after all. The cosmos has spoken.

I urge the chalice we both hold higher, like an offering. Julian's glint of triumph acknowledges my token of surrender. *Go on, finish it, sweetheart.* While he drinks, I slide a hand from under his and slip a packet of powder into his pocket.

Blondie sidles closer. He comes from the right so he couldn't see my maneuver. A good thing because he can't take his eyes off me, he's fascinated. It always begins like this. His eagerness arouses me, but the guy's timing needs work. Can't he see I'm busy? He assumes a purposeful stance, very macho, hands on hips. His tweed coat opens to reveal a gold shield on his belt.

Whoa!

Julian places the glass on my lips like we're sealing a bargain. *Oh, great.* Probably thinks I'm agreeing to his castle idea. He staggers a bit and grabs my bandaged arm. I yelp. He says irritably, "For Christ's sake," and jams the glass against my teeth.

My eyes water, but obedient as a show pony, I lower my nose to the potion. Thinking fast, I nip my own lip before I rear back and stage whisper, "What is this? It smells funny."

Blondie the Cop removes the glass from our mutual grip, gives me a handkerchief and a sympathetic grimace. When he snaps cuffs on Julian, who appears a bit drunk, I manage to look pathetic. Blondie puts his free arm around my shoulders for a quick hug. This bodes well for tenderness in my future.

Or does it? He's looking at me with a Barbie expression, assessing. I'd best watch out.

BIG D, LITTLE D

Pam Clark

The aged stone wall was defaced by a red circle drawn around a stylized ear, both slashed by a diagonal red line resembling a dagger. That and the other graffiti caught Lieutenant Ty Raleigh's attention.

don't piss on deaf pride
fire worthless Worthington
celebrate deaf culture
Deaf President Now!

The nearby uniformed police officer cleared his throat. "Lieutenant, I have the head of security over here."

"Ah...Sturgis, you caught this one, did you?" Ty said, studying the wall. He turned and motioned toward the yellow tape that cordoned off the grassy area in front of the building. "And secured the scene?"

"Yes, sir," Sturgis said, nodding to the two men standing at the corner of the building. "Over there we have Jake Knoll, the head of security. He's the older, athletic-looking guy. And Matthew Cordis, the administrative secretary for the superintendent of the school." Then he hurried back to the wall and began photographing the scene.

That's odd, Ty thought. Sturgis was ambitious, bucking to make detective. He typically hung around during interviews. But this round of questioning wouldn't be business as usual, would it?

The vandalism had occurred on the grounds of the Frederick School for the Deaf—a residential, pre-K through twelfth-grade facility that fell within the jurisdiction of the Frederick City Police. And since two men had shown up to answer routine questions, odds were that one of them was deaf. Most security chiefs would handle things solo. Ty had never conducted an interview through an interpreter, which would probably be Cordis.

He shook each man's hand. "I'm Lieutenant Ty Raleigh."

After a perfunctory nod, Cordis lifted both hands in front of his sweater vest and began signing to Knoll while also repeating Ty's introduction aloud.

Since the campus of FSD was within their call area, all members of the police department took basic signing as part of their training. But it was very rudimentary, just things they'd need in the field. Like, "Is anyone hurt?" and "Can you tell me what happened?" Mostly, the concerned parties wrote back and forth to one another.

Ty figured that Sturgis was hanging back because he didn't trust his signing skills. Lots of cops didn't. Some were antsy about negotiating the Americans with Disability Act or running afoul of local politics, because in some ways FSD was a world unto itself.

When he interviewed for the detective position here, he'd learned about Frederick's sizable deaf population and about FSD. After taking the job he decided to study sign language online. He thought he was fairly accurate, although using the deaf alphabet to fingerspell names was tricky. You never knew when something like that would come in handy, something beyond the basics that the department provided. But he'd kept those skills to himself. That, and the fact that he was fluent in Spanish. It could be useful for folks to think you didn't understand them when they talked amongst themselves.

Not wishing to ignore either man, Ty acknowledged Cordis with a tilt of his head before addressing his remarks directly to the deaf man.

"Let's back up a minute here, Mr. Knoll," Ty said. "I understand that you're in charge of security, but who actually reported the vandalism?"

Knoll began signing his answer and Cordis interpreted.

The process seemed time-consuming and a little unsettling because Ty kept finding his focus ping-ponging between who was signing and who was speaking.

He learned that one of the nighttime dorm counselors had finished his shift around six-thirty a.m. and was heading out to his car when he noticed the graffiti. He'd texted Knoll, then called the cops. Ty noted that Knoll seemed agitated about that call. Probably would've preferred keeping the ball in his court. And no, the counselor hadn't seen anyone hanging around or noticed anything unusual. Since outsiders had been alerted, Knoll had followed the school's protocol and tagged Cordis, their go-to interpreter. They'd both arrived about seven and had been there ever since.

Ty still needed to get a statement from the dorm counselor and check it against Knoll's account. He'd set his partner, Maroni, on that after he arrived. Sturgis had reached the scene within minutes of the call, so he could confirm the arrival time of Cordis and Knoll.

So much for the when. Now for the whys.

Knoll had moved off to shoo away a couple of curious students, allowing Ty to talk to Cordis alone.

Gesturing to the crime scene, Ty asked, "What building is this? Why was it targeted?"

"It's listed on the National Register of Historic Places as the Frye House Field Hospital."

That was as clear as mud. "Because—?"

"Because it was a private residence used during the Civil War to treat wounded soldiers from both sides. Clara Barton supposedly ministered there. Later it was an armory, a silkworm factory, and the staging area for a 1910 expedition to the Arctic before we built our campus around it. As for why it was targeted?" He shrugged. "Probably precisely because it is historic."

After Knoll rejoined them, Ty pitched his next question to both of them. "What can you tell me about the graffiti? What does it mean?" Later he'd ask about who might've put it there.

Knoll had been watching Ty closely while he spoke, and then shifted his attention when Cordis relayed the questions. After a guarded look passed between Cordis and Knoll, Knoll signed his response and Cordis interpreted: "It would be best to continue this conversation in the superintendent's office."

Cordis indicated the crowd of students that continued to gather. "Little pitchers have big eyes."

On the walk over, Ty took note of students milling around and was surprised at how noisy they were, then chagrined at how assumptive that was. Sure, they were deaf, but that didn't make them mute. If some of them were loud, well, they couldn't hear to judge their volume level, could they? But judging from the kids wearing hearing aids, not all of them were totally deaf. Even then, sometimes their speech was hard to follow, like listening to someone with a foreign accent whose syntax was a little off.

Once inside the brick, Victorian administration building, Ty found his partner Matteo Maroni waiting for him. Ty introduced him to the others, then Cordis opened a heavy mahogany door and gestured for the three men to precede him into the superintendent's spacious office. The highly polished, wide-planked wood floor confirmed the building's age.

Cordis addressed the man behind the oversized desk. "Dr.

Worthington, this is Lieutenant Raleigh, the detective assigned to the case. And his partner, Matteo Maroni." As he spoke, he angled himself so he could still sign to Knoll.

Ty stepped forward and shook hands. Worthington was an unremarkable, bespectacled, fifty-something male. But his grip was firm.

"I'm sorry we had to meet under these circumstances," the superintendent said.

"But better than not meeting at all," Ty replied, observing that Worthington both spoke and signed for himself. "Being on campus this morning has revealed how uninformed I am about a significant number of the people I'm sworn to serve."

A sad smile tugged at the educator's lips. "The Deaf community is often overlooked," he admitted. "As evidenced by the fact that this school was built on the farthest fringes of town when it was established in 1869. And that it was the only school to serve the Deaf in the entire state. But please sit, everyone. Make yourselves comfortable while we discuss this unfortunate incident."

Ty took a moment to study the office, admiring the ornately framed etchings of the FSD campus and various Frederick landmarks from days gone by. Many of those depicted the "clustered spires" of the churches made famous in John Greenleaf Whittier's patriotic Civil War poem, "Barbara Frietchie." The city shamelessly capitalized on that fame to pull in tourists, to the point that the department's squad cars were emblazoned with a cityscape of those legendary spires.

While Ty, Maroni and Knoll settled into chairs facing the superintendent, Cordis stood to one side of the desk, hands lightly clasped in front of his midsection. *Interpreter mode*, Ty figured.

"You've doubtless observed the scene," Ty said to the superintendent. "What do you make of that graffiti?"

"I imagine it's a protest against my appointment to this position."

"Oh, why is that? I mean, what underlies the opposition?"

At that, Ty heard Knoll shift in his chair, saw Cordis glance in that direction. A swift glance, subtle, but it was there.

Worthington sighed. "Some people think I don't measure up."

Since silence was often as effective as a question to elicit more information, Ty waited.

"Because I'm only hearing-impaired, not deaf."

"I'm afraid I'm not quite following you, sir. Why is that an issue?"

Knoll shot Ty a look and began signing rapidly, leaving Cordis to interpret: "The detective doesn't know about the Deaf President Now protest at Gallaudet."

It had been the right call to have Cordis interpret for him rather than to sign for himself. Letting these folks talk behind his back had come in handy because he'd just seen Knoll sign something that the interpreter hadn't conveyed—the sign for "obvious." That Ty *obviously* didn't know about Gallaudet's protest. Did Cordis leave it out so as not to insult him, or to protect Knoll? The man had tensed when the superintendent began talking about opposition to his appointment. And Cordis had looked over at Knoll. Maybe the head of security wasn't a fan of the appointment. Or Cordis wasn't. Or both.

"You're right. I don't know anything about that protest," Ty agreed. "But it seems important. Care to enlighten me, Mr. Knoll?"

The man's face became stony and he didn't reply.

Worthington filled the void. "It was back in 1988. At Gallaudet University down in D.C., the college established for the nation's deaf population. Well ahead of the selection of their new president, the Deaf community began advocating for a deaf person to be appointed to the post. All previous presidents had been hearing. However, from the final three candidates that year the board selected the only hearing one."

Oh yeah. A bone-headed move. Ty listened as Worthington

explained the Deaf President Now movement. How students, staff, faculty and even alumni shut down the campus, burned effigies, and marched on Capitol Hill until their four demands were met—the linchpin being the inauguration of a deaf president. It took almost a week, but they were victorious on all four points.

And now those same sentiments had shown up here as graffiti.

Ty pulled in a long breath. "But you're hearing-impaired. Doesn't that make a difference?"

"Our board thought it did, or I wouldn't be here. Actually, the deaf candidate in the final cut took herself out of the running because she'd accepted a similar position elsewhere. But the other applicant and I are both hearing-impaired. I just had more administrative experience."

"And very impressive educational credentials," Cordis added. "Don't sell yourself short, sir. You'll be an outstanding superintendent. This graffiti nonsense will blow over in no time."

Okay, so the admin didn't seem even a little opposed to Worthington's appointment. Or maybe his endorsement was just a lot of smoke-blowing.

On the other hand, Knoll kept his thoughts to himself. Either he wasn't an ass-kisser or he had nothing good to say about his boss.

"Now that we've established why the graffiti showed up," Ty began, "we need to figure who would want it there. Any of you have ideas about who might be responsible?"

Almost in unison all three men shook their heads. Either they really didn't know, or they were stonewalling him.

"Thank you, gentlemen," Ty said as he rose. "I'll be in touch if we find anything. Or if I have more questions."

Maroni spoke up as they headed back to the crime scene. "They weren't much help, were they? Motive, but no suspects."

"It's never easy, is it?"

Hearing faint conversation, Ty looked up to see a pair of workmen chatting as they rolled paint over the scrawls on the water tower that dominated that corner of FSD's campus. He started to say more but his cell phone vibrated. He checked the caller display: Lindsay. *Shit!* Had something happened at school?

"Hey, Squirt. What's up?"

"My ride didn't show. I'm gonna be late to the dentist."

"I'll call you a cab."

"I just checked. None available for ninety minutes. This is Frederick, not Baltimore. Remember?"

He did. That's part of the reason he'd moved them here five years ago. Smaller town, safer. It was also supposed to allow him to devote more time to her. But that wasn't working out so well.

Maroni gave Ty a pitying look and joined Officer Sturgis at the crime scene.

"Are you gonna come pick me up or do I have to cancel? Again."

"I'm headed right over." He killed the connection before she could rag on him any more.

Ty joined the other two men. "Sorry, gotta take some personal time."

"Lindsay giving you grief?" his partner asked.

"Nothing new there." He shrugged. "Maroni…while Sturgis finishes up here, I need you to do a couple of things. Check on the dorm counselor's story, see if it matches Knoll's. Then, see what you can dig up on those three characters we just left. Find out the scuttlebutt about Worthington's popularity, or lack thereof. See if anyone is torqued because he got the job. Like maybe his head of security."

Maroni nodded. "But there's one good thing about this case," he said, gesturing toward the water tower. "At least our graffiti is at ground level." He grinned. "Plus, I don't have to deal with a testy teenager."

Ty grunted. "If I'm lucky she'll give me the silent treatment."

But that wasn't the Lindsay who slid into his car when he collected her from Frederick High.

"Dad, you caught the FSD case. That's so cool! Everyone's talking about it."

"Whoa, I just left there. The department hasn't made a statement and there weren't any reporters on scene. How'd you find out?"

Lindsay rolled her eyes. "It's all over social media. Duh." She pulled out her phone and queued up a picture of Maroni in front of the graffitied wall. "If Maroni's there, it's your case. The whole thing is already trending."

"Can I see that?"

"*May* I see that," she corrected, handing over her cell. "Do you have any leads?"

He studied the photo, grimacing about the potential impact of social media. His boss wouldn't be happy. Or Worthington. To Lindsay he said, "I don't have anything I can share."

She crossed her arms and slumped down in the seat. "Not that you would even if you did."

It was encouraging that she was interested in this case. They hadn't had much in common lately. Hadn't spent a lot of quality time together. When she was little, they'd made a game out of memorizing license plates and recognizing the makes of cars. But after a while his wife had put a stop to that. She wanted to encourage their daughter's interest in her world, the arts. But today his daughter was making an effort to connect with him—an opportunity not to be wasted.

"I'm sorry, Lindsay," he said, pulling out of the school parking lot. "Got lots on my mind right now. I'll come up with some tidbits to share tonight over dinner." Because right now he had bupkis.

***

By the time he returned to FSD things were happening. Sturgis had found an empty spray paint can in the bushes. The color was red, like the graffiti. He'd bagged it and taken it into headquarters to have it dusted for prints, following up on their first real evidence.

Maroni brought him up to speed.

"I questioned Cordis about the head of security, trying to get his take on Knoll. He didn't dish any dirt, but he might not've, even if he knew anything. I mean, Cordis is a company man. All he'd say was that Knoll was old school."

Maroni paused, an uncharacteristic frown crossing his face. "Getting information around here is like pulling teeth. Usually I'd chat up the underlings—janitors, secretaries, maintenance guys—and I did. But Cordis had to interpret for me. It made me feel right stupid."

"There's no need to go there." This situation had to be hard on Maroni, usually such a whiz at information gathering. "It isn't easy to find our footing on such unfamiliar ground."

He shrugged. "But I did find out a few things. Everybody I talked to liked Worthington. He's still new but he isn't coming on like a bull in a china shop. They say he's taking his time, getting to know the place. And Cordis came here with Worthington. Explains why they're so tight. Everyone's bummed about the graffiti, though. Afraid of the bad press it'll bring."

"No surprises there."

"And here's something else. Apparently, there's some sorta hierarchy of deafness, or at least some people think so. Seems that deaf children of deaf parents are at the top of the scale. Our man Worthington isn't. He contracted bacterial meningitis in college, leaving him with a hearing loss."

"People put store in that pecking order?" Ty asked.

"Some do. I got the impression that kids form cliques around it. And since Knoll was old school, I wondered if he had those sorts of prejudices. Asked around about that. But from all accounts he doesn't treat this superintendent any different than the previous one." He shook his head. "Too bad, too. I kinda liked him for the culprit."

"This job's full of disappointments," Ty chuckled.

"Okay, next we—" He broke off and pulled out his phone. "Maroni here." His brow furrowed in concentration then smoothed. "I'll get right on it," he said, ending the connection. "We just got ourselves an anonymous tip. Someone says if we want to know who's responsible for the vandalism, we should talk to the captain of FSD's basketball team, Jacob Jones."

They had to go through the superintendent's office to get permission to speak to the student, but everyone agreed it would be better to do it on campus rather than downtown. Keep it informal. For now. Luckily, the student was a senior, eighteen, so they didn't have to involve his parents. He was happy to cooperate.

Ty, Maroni, and Worthington sat on one side of the conference table in the superintendent's office, and Jacob—a young man resembling Lindsay's favorite rapper, lots of facial scruff and a mop of curly hair—sat on the other. Cordis stayed to interpret, which seemed odd since the student wore hearing aids. *More protocol*, Ty guessed, feeling as unmoored as Maroni had earlier.

"Jacob, thank you for agreeing to talk with us," Ty said, pausing a little as Cordis signed for him. "And that's all we're going to do: talk. You aren't being charged with anything. We're investigating the graffiti incident at the Field Hospital and your name came up. Do you know anything about those spray-painted slogans?"

The student both spoke and signed. "No. They were there when we got up for breakfast."

"Do you have any idea why your name surfaced?"

"No, sir."

"Okay. Do you know why someone would want to cause trouble for Dr. Worthington?"

"Nah. It's lame trash talk, is all. The Super is cool."

"Oh, how's that?"

Jacob looked toward Worthington, a question in his eyes.

"It's okay, Jacob," the man said. "Feel free to talk openly with the detective about our…understanding."

The boy nodded. "The Super cut me and Quinn a break. We were the ones who spray-painted the water tower a coupla nights ago. Someone saw us, called security and old man Knoll caught us. He's fast for a geezer."

"So what happened to the spray can?" Ty asked casually, careful not to tip his hand.

"I tossed it."

"How much paint was left?"

"It was empty. We wrote a lot before we got snagged."

Empty, like the one they were running for prints. "Okay, then what?"

"Knoll said we was gonna get expelled, but it didn't roll that way. We told the Super how come we did it, and he said he sorta understood. That we was…ah, provoked. So, he said to chill and put us on probation. If we stay cool, no harm, no foul."

Ty turned to Worthington. "Provoked how? And why didn't you report this?"

The superintendent adjusted his glasses. "Jacob and Quinn are both members of our basketball team, and one of them has already had some trouble with the authorities. We wanted to keep things in-house. Recently our boys' team was defeated by the local high school. Badly so. There has always been a town-and-gown rivalry. This time the other team taunted our boys as they boarded the bus. Hurled nasty slurs. Especially their team captain. Jacob and Quinn were so angry that they spray-painted the water tower with a slur of their own."

"Yeah," Jacob grinned. "'Fred-neck b-ball team sucks!' Because them fools ain't nothing but rednecks."

Ty tended to agree, but now he was back to square one. Seems the tip had been about vandalizing the water tower, not the Field Hospital.

Ty had just spooned that night's takeout dinner onto their plates when Lindsay started in on him.

"Dad, why can't I get my eyebrow pierced?"

He couldn't catch a break. All he wanted was a quiet dinner, then to disappear into his study and think about the case. Now Lindsay wanted a debate.

Don't overreact, he thought to himself. *She's just being fifteen.* But it took every ounce of willpower he had to keep himself from blurting out, "Because it's a trashy look." *Her mother would've thrown a fit over it.*

Raising an adolescent was tough. It hadn't been so long ago that she'd asserted her independence by eating only orange foods and insisting on wearing her ninja outfit five days out of seven. *That* he could handle. Parenting was much easier when her "whys" referenced everyday stuff. Why is the sky blue? Why do boy dogs lift their leg to pee and girl dogs squat?

Things became much harder when the "whys" moved beyond the empirical to the metaphysical. Why are some people mean? Why do people believe in different gods? The really tough one came when she was ten. The one he could never answer to her satisfaction, let alone his: "Out of all the mommies in Baltimore, why did mine have to get murdered?"

Luckily the eyebrow-piercing question had an easy answer. "If you still want it done when you're eighteen, I can't stop you. Until then, it's a hard 'no.' But I thought you wanted to know about my FSD case?"

She picked up her fork and moved some food around.

"Yeah, okay. We talked about it today in my sign language class."

"Your what?"

She shoved her plate aside, clinking it into her cup of tea. "You never listen to me, do you? I'm taking signing as my foreign language. It's not traditional and stupid, like French or Latin, but it still looks good on a transcript."

She was right. He didn't remember her telling him any of that, promised himself that he'd take more of an interest. Starting now. "Okay. So what've you learned so far?"

Her eyes were wary. Then she tilted her head and shrugged. "A lot of stuff. At first it was all about history. Like how signing got organized into a language back in the day. And how it's the thirtieth anniversary of a bunch of protests about Deaf pride at some college close to here."

Coincidence? Maybe, maybe not. What if there were some basketball players in the class? It was a thin lead, but he'd get a court order for the class roster. Still, Lindsay might know more.

"What else have you learned? Besides how to sign."

"Hmm, that there are two ways of looking at deafness. The one is based on a medical point of view and looks at deafness like some disease or disability that needs to be corrected to make deaf people more 'normal.'" She took a sip of her tea before continuing. "The other one sees deafness as something natural, something unique, kinda like being Native American. That way, deafness is something to be proud of."

"I think I like the second way."

She smiled. "Me too."

Then he saw an opening. "Since you're getting proficient in sign language, would you like to help me out? I've taught myself some signs to use on the job, but I need someone to practice with. Wanna be my study buddy?"

Lindsay crinkled her nose. An expression so like her mother's that his heart stuttered. "Sure," she said. "But only if you don't call it that."

"Okay," he said, laughing.

"You know what, Dad? I kept looking at that graffiti photo when I got home, because something we learned in class kept popping into my head."

"Oh, what's that?"

"That it makes a difference how you spell 'deaf.' Here, I'll show you."

Lindsay left the table and came back with a textbook. "There are two ways. A little 'd' usually refers to not being able to hear, just physical deafness. But a big 'D' refers to Deaf culture." Opening the book, she began to read: "...their beliefs, norms, and values—with an emphasis on Deaf pride."

She pulled up the crime scene photo on her phone and frowned at it. "It doesn't seem right that there's a little 'd' on the sayings like 'celebrate deaf culture,' and 'don't piss on deaf pride.' Like it was written by someone who doesn't know about the Deaf world. Or doesn't care."

He walked over to look at her phone. "Show me."

"Weird, huh?" she said. "It could be sloppy penmanship, though."

"Maybe it's..." He was interrupted by his cell phone. "Sorry, Lindsay. I have to take this."

She went back to eating dinner while he walked to his study, listening to the lab tech's report.

"The results are back on the fingerprints. We have a match to a Jacob Jones, one with a sealed juvenile record. But the dye lot of the red paint match doesn't match the graffiti on the Field Hospital. Sorry, lieutenant."

"No, that might actually be good news. But it means I'll have to interview more high school kids."

It was a tedious day. First, securing a court order for the sign language class list, then matching those names against the basketball team roster and bringing in the two boys.

"Which one are we going to start with?" Maroni asked his partner as they stood in the hallway between the two interrogation rooms.

"The Miller kid. When we brought him in his mom tried to calm him down, but he acted mighty twitchy. The other kid, Forbes, was stone-faced."

"How're you going to work him?"

"I'm gonna start with a bluff. Tell him that we already know he's involved, but if he cooperates, we'll cut him a deal."

It couldn't have gone better, Ty thought to himself. When he confronted Forbes with his buddy's confession, the kid held out for a while. Then his parents started pressing him.

Ty was both grateful and surprised at the parents' cooperation. Not many of them these days had the stones to do the right thing. But they weren't surprised. Seems that sonny boy had long-held issues around deafness. The kid believed that his older brother's deafness had stolen the lion's share of the parents' attention. And now that "asshole" was a BMOC at Gallaudet. Feeling abandoned and resentful, he struck out at a proxy target—Jacob.

Forbes finally broke down after Ty hit him with his buddy's confession. Miller admitted that he lived near the water tower, saw the spray-painting incident, and snatched the empty can after Jacob had tossed it. Miller and Forbes bought their own red paint and targeted Jacob by writing the graffiti and planting his empty spray can at the scene.

In the end the kid was sorry. Sorry that he got caught, not that he did it.

That night's dinner was Ty's specialty, scrambled eggs and sausage. His daughter poured the orange juice while he filled their plates. Neither spoke for a few minutes.

"Without your input, Lindsay, I might not have thought to look outside FSD."

Lindsay's face lit up. Then her expression turned cagey. "Don't I deserve some sort of reward for helping you crack the case?"

"Sure. As long as it's not an eyebrow piercing."

"It was worth a try," she sighed. "Okay, here's what I really want." She paused, bit her bottom lip. "I want to spend a whole Saturday with you."

Ty felt his heart squeeze then swell with pride. "That would be great."

"But I get to choose the activities."

His eyes narrowed. "Such as?"

Her lips twitched with an impish smile. "A day at the spa."

"Whoa, now. I'm not getting a facial or some damn manicure."

She stared him down. "Why not? You'd still be working that case if it weren't for me."

"Yeah, maybe. But come on, Lindsay—"

"Gotcha!" she laughed. "I wouldn't do that to you. But you *do* have to do one thing."

He hung his head. "What?"

"Get a massage. You work too hard, Dad. I want you to relax."

He blinked hard before looking back up.

"Okay," he said. "For you I can do that. While you get a manicure or whatnot." He kissed the top of her head. "Then we'll scoot over to Baltimore and I'll take you out to our favorite restaurant in Roland Park. Deal?"

"Deal." She smiled. "And maybe I'll help you with your signing skills over dinner."

THE CROSSING

Kim Keeline

That morning the traffic snaked more slowly than usual through Tijuana to the San Ysidro border crossing. Four hours of staring at the bumper of the car in front of her. Kris rubbed the grit of the sleepless night from her eyes again and checked the mirror to remove any remaining evidence of tears. She *had* to keep it together. She just wanted to get across the border and not be stuck here anymore. Was that too much to ask?

When the *trapero*, one of the rag men who walked the traffic lines, leaned over her hood and started cleaning her front window, it was a relief to start cursing. She didn't know much Spanish, but she could swear fluently. A tiny blonde American woman who could curse always shocked the locals. When they'd moved to Mexico, Ryan began teaching her Spanish. Naturally, he started by making her memorize every curse word he knew, chuckling as she repeated each one. She had to admit it came in handy sometimes.

She hit the button to roll down the car window and stuck her head out and swore more—with gusto. The *trapero* froze, his dirty rag midair over her window. Meanwhile, his friends helped one of the damned *gaviotas*—freeloading line cutters—through a barrier from a side street.

"*Pendejo*!" Kris swore again, hitting her horn. The *trapero* backed away but the damage was already done. A beat-up Nissan slid into the lane in front of her. She hit her horn again. The Nissan's driver gave her an exaggerated shrug and flipped her off. She swore more and returned the gesture.

A little boy with a cart approached, hoping her open window meant a sale, but she jammed the button to roll it up. He stood there with a water bottle extended for a few seconds. She ignored him. Usually she'd give him a few coins, or at least a sympathetic smile, but today she just wanted this line to move faster. She stared at the Nissan in front of her with a scowl, rubbing her left arm, wincing as her fingers explored the mosaic of red and purple joining the already grey and yellow pattern across her elbow. Her leg probably looked the same under her jeans. That ibuprofen had better kick in or she'd be stiff by the time she got out of the car.

A drip of sweat trickled down her neck and she tried cranking up the A/C. Ryan said he'd fix it, but he'd probably spent the money at a bar instead. Bad enough he hadn't fixed the Corolla's passenger side door he'd broken two days ago. He had dented it pretty badly so it wouldn't lock, but at least it didn't make her uncomfortable like the weak A/C.

Maybe rolling the windows down would be better but she also hated the stink of car exhaust and wanted to avoid being pestered by the vendors. Not that the windows were stopping the fumes.

The line inched forward a car length. Several vendors targeted the stupid line-cheating Nissan in front of her at the same time. An ice cream vendor, pushing a little cart with a bell, tried to join, tipping over the water boy's cart. Immediately an argument broke out, with the boy complaining, and other vendors shouting encouragement or just swearing. Several drivers started honking their horns and Kris joined in. If this got out of hand, it could slow down her lane.

Her passenger door opened. Startled, she glanced up to

find a thin, older man sliding into the seat next to her and closing the door behind him. He was a stranger, dark-haired, disheveled, and menacing. She froze. "What are you doing? Get out of my car!"

The man pulled a gun out of a portfolio case he carried tucked under his arm. The movement was almost casual, like he was offering her some paperwork. The gun's cold black outline filled her vision. Time slowed, as if the gun had stretched the seconds since his arrival in her car to an eternity. Her heart drummed in her ears, drowning out the noises outside the car.

"Don't try anything," the man said quietly, his accent heavy. The gun jerked slightly in emphasis. He kept it low in his lap, out of view of the people in nearby cars but aimed directly at her. The man's hands were steady and the gun shiny in his hands. A car horn went off behind her and she jumped. The rest of the world returned to her vision. She needed to move her car forward a few inches in the line. She did, on automatic pilot.

"What do you want?" Her voice squeaked as she spit out the words between suddenly dry lips.

"Shut up and cross the border," the man snarled.

She was gripping the steering wheel so hard her fingers ached. She forced herself to relax her hold. "I don't want any trouble," she said, her voice sounding high and strained, like it belonged to someone else. "Why don't you just get out and we'll pretend this never happened?" Hadn't a TV show advised that if you were a hostage, try to get the kidnappers to see you as a person? "I'm Kris. I just want to get into San Diego safely."

She automatically rolled her own car forward as traffic moved. Suddenly the border crossing seemed too close. This man could end up shooting her or getting into a gunfight with the officials up ahead.

"Shut up and cross the border. I'm just a friend you're giving a lift to, okay?" He kept the gun aimed directly at her.

Kris looked around. The people behind her apparently hadn't been looking or didn't care that someone had opened her car door and gotten in. Nobody was going to help her. She gave a quick nod of acknowledgement to the man, biting her lip. The cars moved forward another length. She had maybe fifteen minutes before the border.

Her mind ran through her alternatives. She could make a scene. If she yelled or honked the horn would anyone help? Would he shoot her?

She stared at the car ahead of her, considering. The Nissan had a badly dented bumper on the left side, at the spot where a faded sticker for some taco shop was barely legible. What about ramming that bumper? That would serve the line-cutter right and certainly draw attention. It just seemed too risky.

Maybe she could just open her door and run, leaving him there in the passenger seat. Would he be able to shoot her before she could escape?

Kris kept her face forward as if concentrating on traffic but risked a sideways glance at the passenger seat. While his hand was steady, his eyes darted around, and he gasped shallowly like he had run a great distance. Something about the way he sat indicated he might be in pain. Kris remembered how it felt when she had two cracked ribs, the protective way she hunched her shoulders and how it hurt to breathe heavily, as he was doing. If he was injured, it might slow his reactions, which could help. The darting eyes worried her. She needed to calm him down. Panic made people do stupid, dangerous things.

"We'll be at the gate soon. You might want to buckle up and hide that gun or you'll draw a lot of attention to yourself."

He looked surprised, then nodded. "Don't get any ideas." He placed the gun on top of the portfolio case on his lap. With a sharply drawn breath, he reached back gingerly and pulled the seatbelt across to fasten it. The careful way he moved reinforced the idea he was hurt. That didn't mean he wasn't watching her though. The steady hand that placed the gun partly into the open portfolio, while keeping it aimed at her, indicated he was on guard still.

She needed to get him talking. "What's your name? If it comes up at the gate, I need to know."

"Don't pull anything."

Kris's throat was parched but she tried again to make a connection, anything to keep him from firing that gun.

"If I'm supposed to be giving you a lift because we're friends, I should know your name."

"Enrique," he said, "if it should come up." His wrinkled brow was covered in sweat, his eyes watching her but still searching the traffic, as if expecting trouble to come at any moment.

"Okay, Enrique, so you have a passport or something on you, right?"

His head jerked in a quick nod. "Just drive." Clearly not a chatty man.

"I'm driving, I'm driving," Keep it together, she told herself. Don't antagonize him. It would just make things worse. "I'm just thinking ahead to how we'll make this work."

The car slid forward another few feet. This was the slowest border crossing of her life. More sweat was collecting on the back of her neck. Why hadn't Ryan fixed the air conditioning like he'd promised? She didn't dare make a move to roll down the window.

They were just a few cars from the crossing signals now. During the five months she had lived in Mexico, she had crossed frequently, usually when it wasn't so crowded. She missed San Diego, her friends, her old stomping grounds. It had been hard moving down to Mexico with Ryan. It wasn't like she got a lot of quality time with him, after all.

She moved the car forward another car length. They were next to the light.

"Just get us through and it will all be over," said the man

next to her.

She didn't like his ominous tone. She licked her lips, clutching the steering wheel a little tighter to stop the shaking and keeping her eyes on the crossing up ahead. Their turn had arrived.

When the light turned green, she rolled the car forward into the short block for scanning passports and pushed the button for the window. Holding out her passport to the machine, she could feel her heart racing. They would be looking up her info for when she got to the booth ahead.

After a short wait, the second light changed and she pulled up to the immigration booth. A young man stepped out. Kris grabbed Enrique's passport from his outstretched hand and shoved the two passports out the window to the waiting official. The young man took them silently. He glanced at the passports in his hand and then looked at her.

She tried to smile but her face froze into a grimace. The young man glanced at her and then the passport. Then he bent down to look at Enrique, sitting with the portfolio case still on his lap and his hands crossed casually on top of it.

Still leaning over slightly, the young agent glanced down at the two passports again and frowned slightly. "What's your purpose for crossing today?"

Was he suspicious?

"Shopping." It was the first thing that came out.

"And you are from…?"

"I live in Rosarito now. Going back to my old home of San Diego." She was babbling. Did he notice something was wrong?

The young man leaned down a little more to get a good look at her passenger. "And you?"

Enrique gave a wide smile. "I'm helping her shop for a kitchen remodel I'm going to do." It almost sounded plausible. Maybe the agent would believe them.

The border agent looked at her again. Then he nodded. She felt a wave of relief that they were going to avoid a gun battle and held out her hand for the passports.

However, instead of handing the passports to her, the young agent frowned again and said, “Wait here,” and retreated into the booth.

How fast could a heart beat before it failed? She kept her hands tight on the steering wheel and tried to avoid looking at her passenger. She could hear his breathing but she didn’t want to see if his hand was on the gun.

Were they going to be sent to secondary inspection? Would Enrique pull his gun? With all this traffic, you’d think they’d be anxious to get people moving. She stared ahead with longing, wishing her passport was back in the car. Then they could merge into traffic, be on the freeway and away from Mexico.

She couldn’t help it. She had to see what Enrique was doing. She glanced at him carefully. He was shifting uncomfortably in his seat, his face tense. His hands were clenched on top of the portfolio. A jolt of cold ran through the palms of her hands as she clutched the steering wheel. She could practically feel the gun, even though it was still inside the case.

The young agent returned. He leaned down to peer at Kris. She braced herself.

Instead of speaking, he smiled and handed back the passports, waving them on. Kris stared up at him for several seconds before realizing she could go. She dumped the two passports in the center console and rolled up her window as they merged into traffic, slowly navigating the speed bumps and merging lanes.

Once they left the border truly behind them, the road opened up and they hit freeway speed. They rode in silence. Kris glanced at Enrique. He had the gun back out and pointed at her. His lips were curled in a thin smile. She couldn’t decide if that was a good sign. Would he kill her and take her car? Or would he get out and disappear, like he had never forced his way into her life today?

The silence weighed on her. She finally blurted out, “What

now?" She felt pleased her voice sounded calm.

"Just keep driving for a bit. I'll tell you when to pull over."

He looked so damned smug. She'd seen that look on Ryan's face when she'd told the San Diego cops she didn't want their help, the month before they moved. In fact, Enrique's build was a lot like Ryan's. Probably had his same wiry strength, too. She'd have to be careful. She just needed to get away from Enrique and she'd be safe. Home free.

They soon were passing the last of Chula Vista's landmarks and heading toward San Diego.

"Get off here," Enrique grunted. They left the freeway. "Turn right and don't speed." She wanted him to let down his guard, so she followed his directions to the letter. They were heading east, with a few turns here and there, each with a quick direction from Enrique, who seemed to know the area well.

They rapidly left the more heavily traveled streets. Enrique seemed relaxed now but kept his hand on the gun. The area was turning industrial with some patches of open fields and undeveloped commercial lots. The occasional strip malls had faded "out of business" signs. No wonder nobody was walking the sidewalks. They passed fewer and fewer cars. The early afternoon sun beat down on the harsh landscape, with few shadows to relieve the dull, dusty emptiness of the passing neighborhoods.

She felt flushed all over. If something was going to happen, it was likely to be soon. She rubbed at her left elbow and stretched her legs a little surreptitiously to relieve the aches and stiffness. If she needed to move fast, she wanted to be ready.

Suddenly he spoke again. "Turn right here." She turned the car into an apparently deserted alley, lined by the backs of businesses and their dumpsters. Didn't look like the sort of place with security, cameras, or any other help.

Kris considered the possibilities. This could be the time.

She'd have to fight.

"Pull over here," came the order. She stopped slowly, keeping the engine running. Pointing the gun at her, he turned carefully in the seat to face her more directly.

"You did good. I'll get out now. You can pretend you never saw me. I'll just take your cell phone so I can get away before you report anything—and then off you go." He grabbed his passport from the console between the seats.

"You're letting me go?" She could hear the surprise in her own voice. Whatever she had expected, it hadn't been this. She didn't want to give up her phone, but the gun was still right there. He held out his hand for her phone, nodding as if in encouragement. She pulled her phone slowly out of her pocket and handed it to him. He slipped it into the portfolio.

"Look, I'm not a bad guy," he said in a wheedling tone, "just desperate. I couldn't be caught. If you knew what I was running from, you'd understand." Again, the smile. "I don't want to hurt you."

She looked pointedly at the gun in his hand. He smiled wider, putting it in the portfolio with her phone and showing her his empty hands almost like an apology. Chuckling softly, he unbuckled his seat belt. He definitely had sore ribs, slowing him down. He winced as he reached for the door handle, opened the car door, and put one foot down on the pavement.

Now was her chance. She hit the gas pedal. Enrique, just starting to duck out the car door, fell back, his head hitting the car's frame. He tumbled out onto the pavement hard. She stopped quickly and looked back. Enrique lay on the ground behind the car, stunned but still moving, holding his head and moaning.

She put the car in reverse and quickly backed up. The passenger door swung wildly. The thump on the back corner of the bumper and then of the tires going over the man were all gratifyingly loud.

Best to be sure. She stopped and then sped forward, the

passenger door still swinging. More thumps and a cloud of dust. She came to a halt again. He definitely wasn't moving now.

Kris got out slowly. Enrique was sprawled in the alley, the gun and now open portfolio flung out a few feet from him. She circled his body warily. Looking into the case, she was pleased to find a large wad of cash, along with a bunch of financial paperwork and his passport, along with her phone. Maybe the contents would explain what he had been running from. The papers might even be valuable. Why else would he be carrying them? She slipped her phone back into her pocket, glad it hadn't been broken. She had taken a chance, but it had paid off. Money, paperwork—and a gun. Enrique certainly didn't need his weapon anymore. She might. She put it back in the portfolio, placing it on the ground, and turned to face Enrique.

She rolled his body over, searching his pockets but finding very little beyond some change, a folding knife, and a wallet. She stashed everything in the portfolio and shoved it into the already crowded trunk of her car. It wasn't easy to push his body out of view but, luckily, he wasn't a big man. Stashing him between two dumpsters, she looked around to make sure she hadn't missed anything. Still quiet, with no people or security cameras visible. She slammed the passenger door shut and walked slowly around her car.

A warm wave of satisfaction rolled over her. She'd felt the same way early this morning when she'd finally had enough of Ryan bullying her. He'd slapped her across the arm, which he'd already bruised from their argument last night. Or maybe from the fight three days ago? They all blurred together.

She didn't remember picking up the knife. They had been in the kitchen. It had been hot already and she was in shorts and a T-shirt, despite the bruises on her legs. He had broken a bowl at her feet, chips of it flying up and cutting her bare legs. She'd screamed and he'd grabbed her—and the knife block had been nearby. She hadn't thought about it. She'd just struck. And then struck again. And again.

When it was over, she'd cried but then a calmness had come over her. She felt so satisfied. She cleaned up and then packed. She gathered everything of value she could fit in the trunk of her car and headed toward the border. She just hadn't thought about the long lines at that time of the morning.

She'd used his name when they moved in—almost like they were married, he'd said. Nobody really knew her. Now that she had returned to the U.S., she could start her life over again under her own name. Enrique had given her a little cash and protection. It was more than she could have hoped for when she started driving.

At least his little stunt hadn't drawn attention to her at the crossing. Nobody should connect her to the body in their place in the suburbs of Tijuana, especially since she had told the agent at the crossing that she lived in Rosarito. And nobody should connect her to Enrique when they did find him in this alley. They were strangers to each other, after all.

She hopped into the car, carefully adjusting the rearview mirror. As she pulled out of the alley, she felt her tight shoulders loosen. All the pain in her arm and bruised legs faded away. She turned on the radio and adjusted it to a San Diego station and began to hum along softly with the tune.

She should look for an automatic car wash at some point before getting back on the freeway, perhaps? Best not to take any chances. Today was a fresh start and she wasn't going to let anything get in her way.

ACKNOWLEDGMENTS

On behalf of Partners in Crime: The San Diego Chapter of Sisters in Crime, I'd like to thank the following people for their work on our first anthology. When we began the chapter four years ago, I never realized we would come so far, so fast. That's only possible because of a great group of people.

——Kim Keeline
Chapter President, 2019-2020

Kathy Krevat: Our first chapter president and the woman who ushered this anthology through its blind submission process. She put out the Call for Submissions, collected all the entries and made sure they had no identifying info, and got the work out to the editors. She also did the negotiations with the publisher and all the other important setup which made this anthology possible.

Lisa Brackmann and **Matt Coyle**: Our fearless editors had the daunting task of reading all the submissions and choosing just fifteen stories to publish. Then they led those authors through revisions and helped the stories become what you see today.

Rachel Howzell Hall: For agreeing to write the foreword. She knows how to make it look easy.

Martin Roy Hill: Our proofreader/copyeditor went through and made sure this manuscript was ready to go to the publisher.

ACKNOWLEDGMENTS

Down & Out Books: For agreeing to publish this work and for arranging for the terrific cover art.

All the people who submitted: Whether you were chosen for publication or not, we appreciate your submissions.

The readers: That's right, you! If you made it this far, you really stuck with us. Thank you.

ABOUT THE EDITORS

LISA BRACKMANN is the *New York Times* best-selling author of the Ellie McEnroe novels set in China and the thrillers *Getaway* and *Go-Between.* The first Ellie book, *Rock Paper Tiger* was one of Amazon's Top 100 Books of the Year and a Top 10 Mystery/Thriller. *Hour of The Rat*, the sequel, was shortlisted for Left Coast Crime's International Mystery Award and was nominated for the Anthony Award for Best Audio Book. *Dragon Day*, the third novel in the Ellie McEnroe trilogy, was a *Seattle Times* Top 10 Mystery of 2015 and was shortlisted for a Lefty Award. Getaway was an Amazon Best Book of the Month and a finalist for SCIBA's T. Jefferson Parker Award. Her novel *Go-Between is* "a terrific noir tale that channels Richard Stark's stories" and a "Hottest Summer Books" selection from the *Minneapolis Star-Tribune. Black Swan Rising*, her newest book, is about misogyny, mass shootings, and polarized politics, and launched Sept. 8, 2018. Her work has also appeared in *The Wall Street Journal*, *Travel+Leisure*, *Salon*, *Los Angeles Review of Books* and *CNET.* She lives in San Diego with a cat, far too many books and a bass ukulele, and she's playing in a band again after a seventeen-year break.

MATT COYLE is the author of the best-selling Rick Cahill crime novels. He knew he wanted to be a crime writer when he was fourteen and his father gave him *The Simple Art of Murder* by Raymond Chandler. He graduated with a degree in English from University of California at Santa Barbara. His foray into crime fiction was delayed for thirty years as he spent time managing a restaurant, selling golf clubs for various golf companies, and in national sales for a sports licensing company. Writing at night for more than a decade, his debut novel, *Yesterday's Echo*, was finally published in 2013. The wait was almost worth it as it won the Anthony Award for Best First Novel, the San Diego Book Award for Best Mystery, and the Ben Franklin Silver Award for Best New Voice in Fiction. Matt's second book in the Rick Cahill series, *Night Tremors*, was a Bookreporter.com Reviewers' Favorite Book of 2015 and was an Anthony, Shamus, and Lefty Award finalist. *Dark Fissures* (Cahill #3), was a finalist for the Macavity and Lefty awards and was a 2016 Top Pick for bookreporter.com. *Blood Truth* (Cahill #4) was a Shamus, Lefty Award finalist, a Foreword Reviews Book of the Year Silver Award winner for Thriller/Suspense, and a top pick by Bookreporter.com for Best Mysteries of 2017. Cahill #5, *Wrong Light*, was a Shamus Award, Lefty Award and San Diego Book Award finalist. It was also a top pick by Bookreporter.com for Best Mysteries of 2018. *Lost Tomorrows*, Matt's sixth Rick Cahill novel, came out in December. Matt lives in San Diego with his yellow Lab, Angus, where he is writing his seventh crime novel.

ABOUT THE CONTRIBUTORS

LAUREN AVENIUS is a San Diego resident, and Mexican-American California native. Lauren has another upcoming publication, *B is for Bunker* (One Peace Books, 2020).

GRETA BORIS is the author of *The 7 Deadly Sins* novels of psychological suspense. Ordinary women. Unexpected Evil. Taut psychological thrillers that expose the dark side of sunny Southern California. She's the co-director of O.C. Writers and a popular conference speaker. She describes her work (and her life) as an O.C. housewife meets *Dante's Inferno.* You can visit her at GretaBoris.com.

PAM CLARK grew up on Maryland's Eastern Shore in a hometown of 300 people. She earned a Master of Arts in Writing from Johns Hopkins University. In 2016, she won the Book Doctor's Pitchapalooza contest, the American Idol for books, at UNM's Summer Writers' Conference. She is a member of Mystery Writers of America, Romance Writers of America, and Sisters in Crime. Her first mystery novel, *Shoot, If You Must* was published in 2019.

BARBARA DEMARCO-BARRETT'S work has seen print in *USA Noir: Best of the Akashic Noir Series, Orange County Noir, Los Angeles Review of Books, Author's Guild Bulletin, Poets & Writers,* and she's editor of the upcoming *Palm Springs Noir* (Akashic). She hosts Writers on Writing on KUCI-FM. Her book, *Pen on Fire* (Harcourt), was a *Los Angeles Times* bestseller. She was the 2018 president of Sisters in Crime, Orange County Chapter. More at PenOnFire.com.

CORNELIA FEYE is an author, art historian and publisher. She has published three mystery novels, and the first one, *Spring of Tears*, won the San Diego Book Award in 2011. The anthology *Magic, Mystery & Murder*, co-edited with Tamara Merrill, won the San Diego Book Award in 2019. She is the founder of Konstellation Press (KonstellationPress.com), an indie publisher for genre fiction and poetry. Her publications include art historical essays and reviews in English and German.

CHERYL GARRETT started reading mysteries when she was twelve and was given *Nancy Drew and the Hidden Staircase.* She wrote her first mystery five months later. Now as a semi-retired teacher, she has returned to that first love, writing a mystery. She is a transplanted Texan enjoying the mountains of El Cajon with her husband, two cats and two wayward children.

B.J. GRAF lives in Los Angeles. *Sandman* is her third published short story. *Blood Shadows* and *Shikata Ga Nai* came out in the 2019 and 2013 Sisters in Crime Anthologies, respectively, and her agent is currently shopping her near-future-mystery novel, *GENESYS Rx*, featuring the same detectives as *Sandman.* B.J. is also an Adjunct Professor who teaches Film and Classical Mythology at Pepperdine, UCLA, and CSUN. Previously, she worked as vice president of development for Abilene Pictures.

S.J. HAWORTH graduated from UC Berkeley and then worked in publishing in London. Five years later she returned to California to purchase and renovate "a handyman's dream." Marriage took her to Manhattan, Connecticut, Saudi Arabia, Indonesia, Sri Lanka and spots in-between. She wrote for *The Saudi Gazette*, *The Singapore American*, *The Jakarta Post* and various magazines. She finds settling in one place impossible and lives in La Jolla, California, and Naples, Florida.

KIM KEELINE is thrilled to have her first short story also be her first fiction publication. She is writing several mysteries-in-progress, volunteering to drive a 1907 Baldwin steam locomotive, and doing freelance marketing and design, as well as lecturing on history/literature topics. She's a proud member of Partners in Crime in San Diego (the local chapter of Sisters in Crime) and co-chair of the organizing committee for Left Coast Crime 2020: Murder's a Beach. See her work at Keeline.com/portfolio.

KATHY KREVAT is the author of the *Gourmet Cat Mystery* series, featuring a cat-food chef and her demanding cat, Trouble. She also writes the bestselling *Chocolate Covered Mystery* series under the pen name Kathy Aarons. Kathy lives in San Diego with her husband of twenty-seven years in the perfect location—near Philz Coffee and the beach. When she's not writing, she's an advocate for youth arts education and a volunteer for the CCA Writers' Conference, the only free writing conference for high school students. KathyKrevat.com.

MELINDA LOOMIS was born and raised in Southern California. She has at times been an office drone (working in everything from insurance to post-production), culinary student, and unemployed bum. Her work has also appeared in *LAst Resort*, an anthology from the Los Angeles Chapter of Sisters in Crime.

GERALD MARTIN is a beginning mystery writer, and a cantankerous old fart, which helps explain the name of his website—curmudgeonsroost.com. It deals with his three favorite things: writing, cartooning, and sailing. He is working on his first novel, *The Seaborn Scandal*, a mystery in which sailboats play a large part. He lives in Tucson and is actually a pretty nice guy if you're not a politician.

JO PERRY earned a Ph.D., wrote and produced episodic television and raised two children. Her stories appear in *Inkitt*, *Pulp Modern*, *Retreats from Oblivion*, and anthologies. Perry is the author of *Everything Happens* (69 Crime), *Dead Is Better*, *Dead Is Best*, *Dead Is Good*, and *Dead Is Beautiful* (Fahrenheit Press), a series Timothy Hallinan called "one of today's best-written and most imaginative." Perry, her husband Thomas Perry, and their rescue dogs live in Los Angeles.

BARRIE SUMMY amassed student loans and earned degrees in French, Canadian Literature, and Speech/Language Pathology before realizing she wanted to write middle-grade mysteries. She is the author of *The Disappearance of Emily H.* and the *I So Don't Do* mystery series. She is married, has four children and one goldendoodle. She is addicted to licorice. *Manipulations* is her first foray into (writing) adult crime.

CARL VONDERAU grew up in Cleveland. After majoring in economics at Stanford, then dabbling in classical guitar at San Jose State, he ended up with a career in banking. Carl has lived and worked in Latin America, Canada, and North Africa and has managed to put his foot in his mouth in several languages. Carl's first thriller, *Murderabilia*, was published in July 2019 by Midnight Ink.

On the following pages are a few
more great titles from the
Down & Out Books publishing family.

For a complete list of books and to
sign up for our newsletter,
go to DownAndOutBooks.com.

The Swamp Killers
A Novel in Stories
Sarah M. Chen and E. A. Aymar, editors

Down & Out Books
March 2020
978-1-64396-082-1

Timmy Milici, a low-level hitter with the infamous Atlanta-based Duplass crime family, ran off with Melody Duplass to Jacksonville, Florida. Olivia Duplass, her mother and head of the Duplass family, was incensed, and put a price on Timmy—a hundred thousand for his corpse, but with explicit instructions that her daughter not be harmed.

We know that's true. Or, at least, we think we do.

Sixteen writers tell their versions of what happened those fateful days in this gripping novel-in-stories, brought to you from the team behind *The Night of the Flood.*

Driving Reign
The De La Cruz Case Files
TG Wolff

Down & Out Books
April 2020
978-1-64396-087-6

The woman in the stingy hospital bed wasn't dead. The question for Detective Jesus De La Cruz: did the comatose patient narrowly survive suicide or murder?

Faithful friends paint a picture of a guileless young woman, a victim of both crime and society. Others describe a cold woman with a proclivity for icing interested men with a single look.

Beneath the rhetoric, Cruz unearths a twisted knot of reality and perception. A sex scandal, a jilted lover, a callous director, a rainmaker, and a quid pro quo have Cruz questioning if there is such a thing as an innocent man.

Man of the World
Paul D. Brazill

All Due Respect, an imprint of
Down & Out Books
April 2020
978-1-64396-099-9

Ageing hit-man Tommy Bennett left London and returned to his hometown of Seatown, hoping for respite from the ghosts of the violent past that haunted him. However, things don't go to plan and trouble and violence soon follow Tommy to Seatown.

Tommy is soon embroiled in Seatown's underworld and his hopes of a peaceful retirement are dashed. Tommy deliberates whether or not to leave Seatown and return to London. Or even leave Great Britain altogether. So, he heads back to London where violence and mayhem await him.

Coal Black: Stories
Chris McGinley

Shotgun Honey, an imprint of
Down & Out Books
December 2019
978-1-64396-058-6

Set in the hills of eastern Kentucky, these tales lay bare the dark realities of the region. Sometimes the backdrop is the opioid epidemic and all the human detritus and bloodshed that comes with it. Other times it's poachers or petty thieves who take center stage, people whose wild desperation invite danger everywhere they go. High in the hills the action takes place, alongside the rarely seen animals who hunt up there, and sometimes alongside the "haints" and spirits of popular folklore.

Coal Black is a collection of gritty crime stories—cleverly drawn tales with sometimes savage surprise endings.

Made in the USA
Middletown, DE
03 March 2020